SHOA

ARUSSI

FA

HOSIENA ●

KAMBATTA

Kassi Desert

KULU

WALLAMO

BODETTI ●

Mt. Damota
● SODDO

YERGALEM ●

HARAR

Kwoibo Mts.

Mt. Humbo

SIDAMO

no River

GAMO

CHENCHA ●

Lake Abaya

C. Guth

Lake Chama

///////////////////// Wallamo tribal area
– – – – – – – – Provincial boundaries
+++++++++++++++++ Railroad

FIRE ON THE MOUNTAINS

Raymond J. Davis and Dana Maja

Füs.

Fire on the Mountains

The Story of a Miracle —
the Church in Ethiopia

Raymond J. Davis

SUDAN INTERIOR MISSION
164 West 74th St., New York, N. Y. 10023
405 Huron St., Toronto, Ont.

6
DAV-f

Printed in the United States of America

Foreword

This story had to be put in written form. It is the story of missionaries, their trials, their sorrows, their joys, their triumphs. But it is more than that. It is the story of God at work, even when missionaries are removed. True, they were used of God to lay a foundation; they were used of God to pray. True, God raised up Spirit-anointed and dedicated leaders of the national church. But who can account for the revival fires that saw 48 converts become 10,000 in five years — and these, years of foreign occupation of their land?

How do you tell that story? The author has chosen to do it by introducing incident after incident, personality after personality. It is simplicity itself. Men, women and children reveal what God has done. The method is direct — the recitation of personal histories. The end is that the reader sees the variety of people and circumstances God weaves together into the pattern of revival. And, in addition to the cumulative effect of this narrative, is the provision of individual stories that will illustrate messages and enthrall children and adults as they are recited.

The Moody Bible Institute of Chicago has an interest in anything missionary that is true to God. But we have special interest in this story. The names of Walter and Marcella

Ohman, Earl and Pauline Lewis, and the author, Raymond Davis, are written large on our missionary scroll. All former students of this school, we have followed them with our love, our prayers and our concern. And there are other missionary names mentioned in this book which mean much to us, and to the church at large.

Let me introduce my brother, Raymond J. Davis. God has used him in Africa — both east and west. I personally saw him at work in Nigeria in 1957. It is no surprise to me that the Sudan Interior Mission has made him General Director. My brother is as a breath of cool air on a warm day. He is greatly beloved. I thank him for giving us this eyewitness account and the record of the working of God in our own day.

WILLIAM CULBERTSON

Author's Preface

Whenever God's people have learned something of the miracle of modern missions that has been wrought in the mountains of southwestern Ethiopia, their hearts have been filled and their lips have overflowed with praise to God. We have written these lines that many more might know of God's doing in this obscure place.

It is true, in one sense, that we can never analyze the work of God. Jesus talked about the working of God's Spirit in terms of the wind. We do not know its origin or destination; it blows where it wills. We can, however, hear its sound and discover its effects.

To the questions, "Why did all this happen in Wallamo? Why did God choose to do this wonderful thing here?" the ultimate answer is a mystery. The phenomenal growth of the church and the effectiveness of the Gospel in Wallamo can only be attributed to the work of the Holy Spirit. What happened in Wallamo could never have been produced by human effort, however devoted.

Here the wind of God fanned a tiny flame of gospel light. Here the barbarity of men and Satan sought to quench it. Here God found sincere hearts which burned brightly in faith — and the Gospel spread far and wide. Here the fire of God swept over the mountains of Ethiopia.

At the same time, however, there are factors that we can discover. The effects of the wind can be observed. When we try to trace out the pattern of God's working we do not minimize His sovereign grace. We magnify it. As those who are responsible, under God, for the development of a successful strategy of world evangelism, we owe it to God, the church, and the world to investigate the means God used in Wallamo. That is the purpose of this book.

May the winsome characteristics of the Lord Jesus Christ, as found in the lives of born-again Wallamo men and women, encourage others to continue in the proclamation of the blessed Words of Life to every creature.

RAYMOND J. DAVIS

September, 1966
Grand Rapids, Michigan

Contents

PART I
THE FIRE BURNS

1 ~ The Lake of Fire

> *. . . it pleased God by the foolishness of preaching to save them that believe.*
>
> — I Corinthians 1:21

DANA MAJA sat leaning against the wall, half asleep. Others of the group were engaged in conversation, their faces and forms highlighted by the flickering flames of a welcome fire against the chilly night. Then, almost as awaking from a dream, Dana Maja was startled by the subject of conversation. He fought against the stupor of his body's fatigue, and listened more closely. The others were talking about Lake Abaya.

"It is a very strange thing you tell about the lake," offered Lalamo. "Is it really true?"

"I swear by the Emperor's life," exclaimed their host, "it is true! Less than two hours' walk from this very spot, there are holes in the rocks, not far from the shore of the lake. From the holes great clouds of steam rise up, especially in the cold season. It never rests."

Dana Maja leaned forward, "What's that? Hot water and steam coming up out of the ground? Where does it come from? Is there no fire?"

13

"If my guests were not so weary, I would take you this moment to see the place. If you choose, tomorrow morning as you begin your journey, I will take you there and you may see for yourself. It is better that we do it in the daylight. In the dark it is frightening."

Soon the fire died down and sleep overcame them one by one. All was quiet now and dark. Dana Maja did not like what he had heard. *If it is hot enough to cause the water to steam, there must be fire,* he thought. *Another description of a lake of fire seems more than a mere coincidence. Very well, I will take a look at it in the morning.*

But morning was a long time coming. Tossing and turning Dana Maja could not sleep. The words of that one, Wandaro, kept going through his mind, coming back again and again. He could not erase the frightening picture from his thoughts. *I should never have listened to him,* thought Dana Maja. *There was something peculiar about him the first time I saw him. I should never have paid any attention to him.*

Wandaro *was* different: naive, yet bold and uninhibited. Dana Maja was accustomed to people, especially strangers, approaching him with timidity and fear, sometimes nervous and reticent, for he was a great man, a chief,* and the owner of many slaves — some Wallamo, some of other tribes.

He had been down in the lowlands looking after his interests in a cotton farm when a poorly clad stranger had intruded in a most unusual manner. He had come up to Dana Maja and spoken abruptly yet sincerely. "Godo (master), you will die some day, and if you do not repent and believe on Jesus Christ before you die, you will go to hell. You will burn in the lake of fire which never goes out."

The chief had not wanted to listen, but it was too late. He

Dana in Wallamo indicates a chief of a small area. Several *danas* would be subject to a higher chief.

knew that he was a wicked man and often he had asked himself the question what would happen should he die. Beckoning to the man to come closer, he asked him to tell him more of this matter. Wandaro clearly and simply witnessed to Dana Maja of his need of salvation and the willingness of Jesus Christ, God's Son, to forgive him his sin. When Dana Maja asked the whereabouts of this person upon whom he should believe, Wandaro told him that He was now in heaven. He would return some day, perhaps soon, and Wandaro described how He would take all those who had believed on Him to that wonderful land.

Weeks and months had passed since Dana Maja had first heard of the lake that burned with fire, but it had often been recalled to his mind. Yesterday he and Lalamo had started out on a trading trip, heading south from his home about 10 miles from Soddo. They had traveled almost 20 miles when evening came, and had stopped near Lake Abaya for the night. How strange to hear in this place of steam coming from the ground — and beside a lake! The thought troubled him greatly and he could not sleep.

Dawn came at last. Wearily Dana Maja joined the others and climbed into his saddle. His body ached. The cold wind bit deeply into his bones. Only the sound of the animals' hoofs on the rocky pathway broke the silence.

Ahead the sun was rising over the hills across the broad lake. It shone in a path of flaming red on the water.

The sun on the lake looks like fire, thought Dana Maja, *Why must everything remind me of that man Wandaro's story? Could a lake like this really burn?*

There it was! Just in front of him, clearly visible in the early morning light, were rocks — black, gray, strangely shaped rocks. And around them steam was rising out of the ground.

"How long has this been going on?" inquired Dana Maja.

"Who knows? It has been forever as far as we know. We have always heard talk of an unceasing fire. Just yesterday I was speaking with an old man and he told me that these steaming holes are becoming more numerous year by year. He said it may some day reach down to the edge of the lake itself. When this happens, according to him, perhaps all the water in the lake will begin to boil and steam. But — what do I know?"

Bending down the men placed their hands on the rocks. They felt warm, even hot. The steam which now blew in their direction as the wind changed smelled strangely, and they quickly drew back in fearful apprehension.

Dana Maja slowly shook his shaggy head in disbelief. "I can't believe it." Others in the party chattered nervously, but Dana Maja, evidently deeply impressed, was silent and quickly turned to mount his mule and ride away.

Heat, steam, boiling water — you cannot have these without fire. No fire did I see, but without doubt there must be fire very near, down in the earth. Eye-ko-ba (it doesn't matter), *I'll stay away from this place and perhaps no harm will come of it.*

He dug his heels into his mule's sides, and the mule clattered back along the road they had just traveled. He would forget this thing and continue his trading journey.

Not long after Dana Maja's brother became ill. In desperation they took him on a stretcher the ten miles to the mission clinic at Soddo, where a nurse treated the sick man for dysentery.

"Are you a believing person?" the nurse asked Dana Maja. "If I give you medicine for your brother in this bottle, will you bring the bottle back?"

"Yes," replied Dana Maja, even though he knew in his heart the answer to both questions was *no*.

While he was waiting for the nurse to prepare the medicine for his sick brother, Dana Maja and the others listened as a white man spoke to them. This man mentioned the name of the same person of whom Wandaro had spoken. Strangely too, this man said that one day this Jesus would return from heaven and take all who knew and loved Him away with Him. For the others who were left behind because they did not know Him, there would be only judgment and the lake of fire.

As soon as he had the bottle of medicine in his hands, Dana Maja hurried away. When the medicine was finished, it became necessary to return to the mission for another supply. Dana Maja had heard that the white people did strange things and he felt he needed some protection against whatever evil influence might be there. Commonly, the Wallamos sought and used "charms" to ward off the ill effects of other people's magic or unknown power. He had often himself made sacrifices to Satan and believed in the efficacy of fetishes. He wondered what he could do now to counteract the evil influence of the white man.

Perhaps since the foreigner did not use tobacco, some of that might prove a good charm, he thought. Putting a handful of tobacco leaves in his pocket he hoped that it would somehow offset the dangers of another visit to the mission. Somewhat more confident he returned to the missionary nurse for more medicine. Strangely enough, it must have worked, for nothing happened to him.

For several months life went on as usual for Dana Maja.

2 ~ Dana Maja's Decision

And he trembling and astonished said, Lord what wilt thou have me to do? And the Lord said unto him, Arise, and go into the city, and it shall be told thee what thou must do.

— Acts 9:6

"THIS IS IT! This is it!" Dana Maja cried loudly. "This is what Wandaro said was going to happen! The terrible noise, the earth shaking, the fire, the smoke! This is the time of God's judgment. It must be this Jesus has come back to earth!"

Dana Maja lay trembling with fear in a shallow gully. Early that morning he had started on his way from his home to Soddo town. Paying little attention to the trail or the sights around him, he had been lost in thought. The mule had seemed to sense his master's wishes and was hurrying him along to his destination. For several minutes an unfamiliar sound had been buzzing in his ears almost unnoticed. As it had grown louder and louder, he had finally become aware of this strange noise. Lifting his face to the sky he was startled to see a shape moving in the air. But he had had no time to ponder the strange sight.

18

At that moment the earth had begun to shake. The heavens rumbled like thunder, great flashes of fire like lightning lit up the sky, rocks were thrown into the air and the very earth seemed to erupt. The mule, startled by the strange and fearful noises, had bolted, throwing its rider to the ground where he now lay, his heart pounding madly in fear.

For what seemed like hours the awesome sounds continued. But presently it became quiet, and Dana Maja rose dizzily to his feet. The proud chief was now a pitiable sight — clothes disheveled and covered with mud, fear and anxiety written all over his face. With difficulty he caught and mounted the mule. There was only one thing to do. He must as soon as possible believe in and follow this Jesus. If Jesus had come, he probably wouldn't stay in Wallamo very long, and Dana Maja wanted to get ready to go to heaven with Him. He needed someone to tell him what to do.

Urging the mule forward he hurried to the home of a Christian man whom he knew lived nearby. Labanya Godo was not there but his wife was. When she saw the chief coming she recognized him with fear. "I can't let him in," she said to herself. "I can't let him know where my husband has gone. He must be out after more slaves." Although she knew that her husband had gone to a baptismal service, she was too afraid to tell Dana Maja of this. Her only response was, "I don't know where he is."

Dana Maja left the house. Farther down the path he saw a group of people. "Where are you going?" he called to them. They were going to the baptismal service, but they also hesitated to tell him. One of them was Labanya Godo who said to his companions, "The Lord didn't turn away from one sheep after the ninety and nine were in. Why should we refuse to witness to this man just because we are fearful? We must tell him about Jesus and His work for us." And he did so, there on the path. Then he added, "We are going to a baptismal service. Come along with us to watch." The chief agreed.

Arriving at the stream, Dana Maja saw large groups of people gathered on both sides to watch. The chief stood with the crowd, watching eagerly to see what the Christians were doing. This was the first time he had been to a baptismal service. Just as they arrived some who had been his slaves in the past but had run away were being baptized. Some of them recognized the chief in the crowd and were afraid — he might be there to take them back into slavery. So they climbed out on the other side of the stream. But Dana Maja did not seem to notice who was being baptized. His mind was too greatly agitated and disturbed by the events just past.

Then everyone went to the home of one of the elders for the communion service. This would be the first communion for those who had just been baptized. The unbaptized believers sat down outside the house to wait, Dana Maja among them. He was angry. He wanted to see what was going on inside but was being ignored.

Suddenly he said to himself, "Am I not a chief? Why should I sit here outside? I will go into the church as a chief should." But he found that he couldn't get up off the ground — his knees had lost all their strength. He tried again. Nothing happened. It was terrible, not to be able to get up, and all the time he sat there others were inside the church apparently putting something into their mouths. But he was still sitting outside when the service ended and the people came out.

By this time the presence of the chief was known to everyone. The pastor with the elders and Labanya Godo came up to Dana Maja, telling him how wonderful it was to know Jesus Christ as their Saviour and to have His joy and peace in them at all times.

One of these men was Wandaro.

"Saro, saro, (peace, peace) have you spent the day in peace?" asked Wandaro.

"Peace? Where in times like these will one find peace? This day I have not known peace. In fact, today for the first time in all my long and wicked life I have been afraid," cried Dana Maja. "Tell me, Wandaro, did Jesus Christ return?"

"No, Dana Maja, Jesus Christ has not yet come back, but it may be He will come very soon," answered Wandaro eagerly. "If Jesus Christ had come back you would not see me nor these others here. He would have taken us to heaven with Him. It is well for one to believe on Jesus and be ready for Him when He comes, Dana Maja."

By this time Dana Maja and Wandaro, with Labanya Godo, had started down the path toward Labanya Godo's home.

"And what was it that I saw today as I traveled toward Soddo? I heard this great noise and looked up into the sky. There was this great thing flying through the air, nothing pulling it, nothing pushing it. My mule, the fatherless brute, bolted and threw me to the ground. The earth trembled, dirt and rocks flew into the air, trees and houses crumbled before my eyes. Did you not hear, did you not see these things?"

"Yes, we saw it, we heard it. We too were afraid, but we knew this was not the coming again of Jesus Christ," replied Wandaro. "These are only the machines of war that the invader of our country* uses to overcome our king and country. The enemy can fly through the air. Sometimes they get into their small iron houses and run along the ground as fast as a horse, shooting their guns from the windows and doors."

But the chief was too fearful and perplexed to comprehend their words. It was necessary to quiet him down before they could hope to help him understand the Gospel. When they

*The Italian invasion of Ethiopia was well under way before nationals in the interior knew it had begun. Dana Maja was converted in 1936, probably toward the end of the year.

*Dana Maja today
is the leader
of all the Wallamo churches.* SIM

Christians listen to preaching outside a small church. Niger-Challenge Press

Washing feet after a dusty trek is a refreshing Wallamo custom.
Niger-Challenge Press

got to Labanya Godo's home, warm water was brought and Labanya Godo washed the chief's feet. They cleaned the mud from his clothes and kindled a warm fire. His wife brought them steaming cups of salted Wallamo coffee. It was not long before the chief relaxed and appeared ready to listen.

Yet as he thought back on his ride, Dana Maja shuddered visibly. Never before in his life had he been really frightened. The owner of more than a hundred slaves, he had often raided and robbed. He had had many narrow escapes, but never before had he been so terrified. The haunting memory of the lake that burned with fire had not been far from his mind since that day, months ago, when Wandaro had first told him about it. Here, too, was something far beyond the power that he, Dana Maja, possessed. It was a very subdued chief who spoke to Wandaro softly, almost pleadingly.

"Wandaro, are you not afraid? Does not all that we have seen and heard today turn your stomach to water? Why are you and your friend, Labanya Godo, both of you common, ordinary men, not alarmed or anxious at all?"

"True, Dana, we are sometimes afraid when we see and hear of these things of the Italian armies, but we have peace and calm in our hearts because our trust and our confidence are in God. We know that His Son, Jesus Christ, has saved us and that He will take care of us."

Wandaro leaned forward earnestly and peered into the eyes of the chief. "You, too, can have peace."

"I am tired of struggling, Wandaro," answered the chief. "I care not for the machines of death. What I want to know is, is there room for me in the House of God?"

Wandaro's eyes glistened with joy as he stood abruptly to his feet. "Labanya Godo," he exclaimed, "get the book. Read to us about the ruler who came by night and knelt at Jesus' feet. The chief wants to do the same!"

And so that night Dana Maja, chief, slave owner, mighty man, came to Jesus Christ humbly to take Him as His Saviour.

Dana Maja came to the Lord, as the Wallamos say, with both hands, wholeheartedly. Being by nature a leader he was fitted for responsibility. The people came to have great confidence in him, willingly accepting his leadership.

Before his conversion late in 1936 his contact with missionaries was slight. He himself attributes his conversion to Wandaro's testimony. And the missionaries left the country without having met Dana Maja, the believer. So he stands as a symbol of what God did through a handful of simple Christians, with little or no outside help. Though they had little teaching, they obeyed what they had.

Dana Maja today is the leader of the whole Wallamo church.

PART II
THE FIRE LAID

3 ⤳ Unlocked Secrets

This is the way, walk ye in it.

— Isaiah 30:21

In the month of March, 1928, a long, heavily laden caravan wound its way up and over the rim of the saucer in which lies Addis Ababa, capital of Ethiopia. It was traveling no particular road, for there were no roads in the true sense of the word. To travel in any direction from the capital, one followed narrow trails, deep-dug ruts carved from the rock and hard clay surface, that twist and wind between rocky knolls and peaks and grassy meadows out of the valley to the gently rolling land beyond. Multitudes of people, mules, horses, donkeys had plodded these routes for centuries.

The caravan, under the direction of Dr. Thomas Lambie, had the far-distant town of Jimma in western Ethiopia as its destination. Dr. Lambie, a medical doctor and missionary of long experience, was one of the original trio (Rowland Bingham, Alfred Buxton and himself) to whom had come, not long before, the vision of opening up the southern provinces of Ethiopia to the Gospel. So it was that he now found himself leaving his hospital in Addis Ababa and moving out into unknown territory at the head of a caravan.

27

Looking back on the caravan from the front, one could scarcely see its tail straggling far behind. Its sixty-six mules, twenty donkeys, nine horses, twenty-five head carriers, twenty-two mule drivers, plus personal servants stretched out about a quarter of a mile. The mules and donkeys carried the tents, camp-cots, provisions and personal belongings. The muleteers did the packing of the animals, while the head carriers carried those loads which could not be packed on animals or were too fragile. The nine horses were for Dr. Lambie and the missionaries accompanying him: Mrs. Lambie and their young daughter Betty, Mr. and Mrs. George Rhoad and their small son George, and the three single men to whom Dr. Lambie sometimes referred as the C.O.D. boys — Glen Cain, Walter Ohman, and Clarence Duff.

Jimma was about 200 miles from Addis Ababa by trail. Normally a caravan could cover fifteen to eighteen miles in a day — but normal days were rare on the trip. Their guide was an Ethiopian who swore that there were no trails in the entire country that he did not know intimately. In a few days, however, Dr. Lambie became aware that the party was *not* on the route to Jimma but was traveling almost straight south. Nevertheless, he decided they should continue on this trail until they reached a district known as Kambatta. There the trails to the west and the south divided, and the party could turn westward crossing the Omo river to reach Jimma.

In Hosiena, the capital of Kambatta Province, Dr. Lambie met Dejazmatch Moshesha,* the Governor, whom he had known previously in western Ethiopia. The hospitable Ethiopian people insisted that Dr. Lambie and his party stop for a time of rest to refurbish the caravan and visit with the Governor. Dr.

Dejazmatch is Amharic for General. The Governors of the various districts and provinces are Amharas, the ruling tribe in Ethiopia, and are appointed by the Emperor.

Range after range of mountains greet the traveler in southern Ethiopia. SIM

Dr. and Mrs. Tom Lambie traveling through Ethiopia. Davis

Trails are steep and the going is rough even for mules. SIM

Loading a mule with tent and bedroll for the trek is hard work. Davis

Lambie's reputation as a medical doctor had traveled far and wide, and there was much work to do, including help for the Governor's family. Moshesha put great pressure upon Dr. Lambie to stay in Kambatta and start a clinic, but he insisted, "No, our permit is for Jimma."

Actually they had no permission to start work anywhere. Their letter of permission to leave the capital stated that their trip was to be in the nature of an exploratory visit to the interior, and a literal rendering of the letter gave them "permission to take the air." At this time Dr. Lambie learned that another friend of his from earlier days, Dejazmatch Igazu, the Governor of Wallamo Province, was ill and needed medical care. So the party moved on southward, and after several days' travel reached Soddo, provincial center of Wallamo. Word of their arrival had preceded them, and they were regally welcomed — in the style usually reserved for a victorious army.

The Governor of Wallamo also invited Dr. Lambie and his people to remain and work in his area. In view of the total absence of modern medical help in these provinces it was not surprising that the governors should desire so capable and kindly a man as Dr. Lambie to stay with them. The missionaries were aware, however, that another important person lived and ruled in the neighboring province of Sidamo — Dejazmatch Biru. According to Ethiopian custom and courtesy it was unthinkable that such prominent guests as the Lambie party should be in the area and not visit his court. Since the journey to Yerga Alem, capital of Sidamo province, required several days' travel eastward, Dr. Lambie and Clarence Duff left the rest of the party in Soddo while they made the journey. The Governor welcomed them warmly and lavished them with gifts. He, too, urged them to remain with him.

In their negotiations with the Regent Ras Tafari (who became Emperor in 1930, taking the name Haile Selassie) before they left Addis Ababa, he had stated that he was not in a position to give them full permission to establish missionary work outside of Addis Ababa. But if any of the governors encountered on their journey desired them to locate in their areas, it would be acceptable to him. With the Regent's words in mind, the leaders of the party were deeply impressed by the repeated invitations of these governors. They wondered if perhaps God, in His own marvelous way, was directing them to stay in these areas rather than to go on to Jimma, where they had no assurance of a similar welcome.

The Governor of Wallamo was delighted when the missionaries decided to stay. He showed Dr. Lambie and Mr. Rhoad a beautiful hilltop site at the foot of Mount Damota, overlooking a broad valley. There was a good water supply nearby, and he suggested this as a site for the mission station. The conviction grew stronger day by day that, whereas Jimma had been their planned destination, God had in His overruling providence brought them to Wallamo. Like the Apostle Paul, they "assuredly gathered that the Lord had called us for to preach the gospel unto them" (Acts 16:10).

It was one thing, however, to be royally welcomed to the Governor's court in Soddo — a town built by the governing Amharas as an administrative center. It was quite another to earn a welcome from the Wallamo people on whose land the mission station would be built. For although the Governor, an educated Amhara and member of the Coptic Church, had invited them to stay and had given them the land, the missionaries would be working, not primarily among the Amharas, but among the more primitive Wallamo tribe, whose language had never been reduced to writing.

On a foothill of Mt. Damota, a mile from Soddo, known by the Wallamo people as Otona, several houses were built in mud and wattle style with grass roofs. (During the rainy season, the grass used to bind the mud plaster began to sprout!) There was no glass for window panes, and unbleached muslin formed only a partial solution to the need for privacy. Nor did it do much to keep out the cold winds which blow twelve hours of the night nearly all year round. For Soddo lies at an altitude of about 7,000 feet, and the nights are cold.

The lack of privacy actually helped the missionaries in their first task — learning from the people their very interesting and expressive language. As the brown-skinned, thin-boned Walla-mos crowded the premises and carefully observed every action of the missionaries, they chattered and exclaimed to one another. "Haga-aibi! Haga-aibi!" they would say as every new item was unpacked from trunks and boxes. "Haga-aibi!" Their brown eyes would open wide, and their eyebrows lift, furrowing their foreheads under thatches of curly black hair.

The missionaries soon decided that the Wallamos were asking, "What is that?" about each new article. When they tried the phrase out themselves, pointing to an object and asking "Haga-aibi," they received a different answer for each object. In this way a list of nouns was made up.

Walter Ohman and Clarence Duff visited in the homes of the Wallamo people every day, sitting and listening to the talk, although they didn't understand a word they heard. But the Africans appeared anxious for them to learn their language, and patiently repeated simple phrases. Evenings the two men spent comparing notes on the day's new words and phrases.

Tribal languages, contrary to the layman's concept, have well-defined rules of grammar. Often the more isolated the tribal group, the more pure and regular its language. In Wal-lamo, however, there was no possibility of asking anyone a question on the grammatical construction of a sentence. Even if the missionaries had been able to converse with a Wallamo-speaking person, the informant would not have been able to state the rule, since the grammar of their own language was unknown to them. Having learned their language as children, they spoke it correctly without knowing why they said it in this form or that.

One by one the secrets of the Wallamo language were unlocked through perseverance, patient plodding and much prayer. Long before they were able to know why it was said a certain way, the missionaries were able to speak simple phrases to the people and to understand something of what was said in reply.

The work of constructing the buildings was finished in August, 1928, and a month later Clarence Duff left Soddo to open work among the Kambatta people. Glen Cain had already left with Dr. Lambie to begin work in Sidamo.

4 ~ *Opportunities*

. . . the things which happened unto me have fallen out rather unto the furtherance of the gospel.

— Philippians 1:12

"WHAT DID YOU SAY was the name of that man?" The old woman stood anxiously looking up into the face of the missionary.

"His name is Jesus."

"You said if we believe in this Name He will help us?"

"Yes, if you believe in Jesus and call upon His name you will be saved."

Selma Bergsten mounted her mule and began to move along the path toward home. She had gone only a short distance when she heard the woman's voice behind her. Turning in the saddle she saw the woman running down the trail.

"What is that name? Please be patient, I can't remember what you told me. Tell me again."

Once more she was told. But it was growing late and the missionary was in a hurry to get home. She touched her heels to the mule and once again started down the path.

"Wait, wait, wait! I want to call my son. I am old and I

forget quickly. Wait till I call my son. Then when I want to call upon that Name, he will remember what it is."

Selma Bergsten had come to Soddo in 1929 along with Mr. and Mrs. Earl Lewis and Ruth Bray, a nurse. This brief incident seemed to be typical of the Wallamo's reaction to the good news about God's love for them in Jesus Christ. None of them had ever heard the Gospel before. They were living as their fathers for generations had lived — in fear and superstition. The only way the light of the Gospel would shine into their darkness was for the missionary to go and tell them.

It soon became apparent that one of the best times to visit the people was at a funeral. Funerals were important events in the life of the Wallamo people. It was unthinkable for a Wallamo who was at all able to travel not to attend the funeral of a friend or acquaintance, though it required miles of travel on foot. At the mission station the sound of loud wailing and singing could be heard almost constantly, sometimes from a great distance.

One evening two of the lady missionaries walked to a nearby family area (four or five houses built close together) to express their sympathy, since it appeared from the actions of the people that a death had occurred. As they approached the home they saw great numbers of people weeping and wailing. Ushered into the large grass house, and seated as honored guests, they expressed their condolences. To their consternation, they learned that it was not a person who had died — but a cow!

When sufficient time had elapsed for them to excuse themselves, the two ladies found that preparations were already made to provide a meal for them. By then it was near dusk and very dark in the hut — so dark that it was impossible to see what they were expected to eat. But that was not all. The Wallamo people are most hospitable, and in their desire to show even greater

Curious and skeptical Wallamos watch the missionaries and their strange activities. Füssle

Pagan Wallamos eat their meat raw with a knife. Füssle

A Wallamo woman makes cornbread on a griddle. SIM—R. Reimer

honor and courtesy to their guests, they took the food in their own fingers and put it into the mouths of the missionaries — who had no idea what they were eating. They just knew it didn't taste good.

Later the missionaries learned that it was plantain or wild male banana — one of the basic foods of the Wallamo people. To make it edible, the Wallamos scrape off the lower part of the fibrous leaf and collect the pulp in a receptacle. This receptacle or vat may be considered the Wallamo refrigerator. A hole is dug in the ground into which the vat is put. The pulp is then worked to a firm consistency by the women who mix and mash it with their bare feet. After that it is covered with leaves from the banana plant and allowed to ferment for several months. When it is properly cured, it is cut up into pieces and baked.

Most of the missionaries did not find the "bread" very appetizing, but the lovely characteristics of the Wallamos' hospitality and friendliness soon won their hearts. The willingness of the missionaries to eat the Wallamo's food in their homes with them was a great factor in the opening of their hearts to the message the missionaries had come to bring.

Within two years the missionaries had learned enough of the language to be able to give a simple Gospel message. As their proficiency in the language grew, they also began to learn something of the origin and traditions of the Wallamo people.

"We used to live in Kindo," they were told, "to the west, near the Omo River. We were few people then, but we became more and more. Then a king came who had many sons. He sent them out to take new lands. The princes called these lands after their own names — Kulo, Gamo, Gofa, Wolita, and many more. From their descendants came the different dialects of the Wallamo tongue.

"Soddo? Soddo belonged to the Marakos [the Wallamo name for the Hadiya and Gudeila tribes]. The great king's oldest son was Damota. He became ruler of the Wallamo people in Kindo after his father. He made all of his brothers' new countries into one great kingdom. To increase his kingdom, he came east from Kindo with many warriors, and drove out the Marakos from Soddo, Otona, Dalbo. This mountain here above Otona — he conquered the fortress there and called the mountain after his name — Mount Damota.

"After this the Sidamo and Arussi Galla people who lived east of Soddo and by Lake Abaya were driven out and across the Balatie river, to Sidamo.

"This was many generations ago, but it is true that you can see the grave of King Damota in Kindo. It is a sacred place. Warriors with spears and shields guard it at each corner of the big mud wall around it. All day and all night they are there."

With their increased language ability, Walter Ohman and Earl Lewis had been able to establish friendly contacts in many villages surrounding Soddo. From the very beginning the Wallamo people were interested in the Gospel, but they were steeped in demon worship, and gripped by the regular worship of Satan. The common people lived in constant fear of evil spirits and of the witch doctors who exercised considerable control of their lives.

When some began to show active interest in following Christ, opposition took tangible form. The missionaries noticed that those who had been friendly were one by one staying away and avoiding them. It took some sleuthing, but they finally learned that the witch doctor was causing the people to stay away. He was telling them that the missionaries were four-eyed people — because Mr. Lewis wore glasses. Four-eyed people, the witch doctor said, would eat Wallamos and send their blood back to their own country!

When it became clear that this was a primary factor in the opposition, Walter Ohman and Earl Lewis went to visit the man who was the chief instigator of this story. "Come to our homes," they said. "Look into every corner of our houses. Inspect everything we have." The man was too much afraid to come voluntarily, but they cajoled and shamed him into coming by appealing to his manhood. When he finally did come, shaking and trembling with fear, they offered him food and showed him through the rooms of the houses, under the beds, behind and inside boxes. His visit dispelled a good many of the fears of the people.

There were other barriers to be overcome, however. As the missionaries traveled among the Wallamo people they observed that some houses were different — they had two doors instead of one. These houses, they were told, belonged to the devil, a fact which explained another aspect of the Wallamo's fear. Because the missionaries' houses had two doors, one in front and one in the rear, the people were suspicious and wondered at this seeming coincidence.

The worship of Satan was well organized among the Wallamos and followed a prescribed ritual. The many different sacrifices were somewhat similar to offerings in the Old Testament. On the first day of the year they conducted a celebration that remotely resembled the Jewish Passover. Instead of being a sacrifice to God, however, it was a sacrifice to the devil. A bull would be killed as a sacrifice, and its meat divided among the four or five houses in a family clan. The blood of the bull was caught in a gourd and then sprinkled on the door-posts of the house. A spot of blood was put in the middle of the forehead of each member of the family, and the meat was divided among each member of the household, so that every person got a part of each organ. The ceremonies were conducted so that at sundown the head of the household would be on his knees with hands outstretched, praying to the devil. Then the meat-feast began, with the meat eaten raw.

"Who is going to draw your water?" the workmen asked.

"We will draw it ourselves," Earl Lewis replied.

"Well, who is going to hoe your garden? Who will pasture the cattle? What about your food?"

"We can do and have done all of these things. And since we do not have money to pay you to do them now, we will gladly do them ourselves. True, there will not be much time left to go among the people to tell them about Jesus, and for this we are sorry."

The 1929 Wall Street crash, which ushered in the depression, had far-reaching effects, touching the lives of people all around the world. A substantial part of the support of missionaries was swept away, including those in Ethiopia. When they were asked whether the work should be curtailed and new workers not sent out until sufficient funds were available, the missionaries all said "No." They would be happy to share whatever was available and would trust God to provide.

There had been no money sent them for several months when the missionaries at Soddo decided to give notice to the Wallamo men and boys working for them. They came to this decision reluctantly, for it had been hard to get workmen in the first place. Almost all Wallamo men farmed the fields around family houses. They had to be able to pay the Amhara overlords for use of the land. In the dry season between crops, and in the months between planting and harvest, workmen were always available. But when their farms needed them, none were to be found or else only young boys who could be spared from farming.

Still, Mr. Lewis and the others felt that it was hardly right to ask the Wallamos to work for them "on faith" even though they themselves would be living that way — without any assured income. So the men were told that at the end of the month their services would no longer be required, since there was no money to pay them.

The announcement was a great shock to the workmen. Up to this time they had refused to believe that the missionaries were not in government service and being paid by the government. (This was not too surprising, since the Governor had invited the missionaries to stay and had given them the land for the station.) Now they looked at one another in amazement, forced at last to believe what the missionaries had always told them — that it was God Himself who had sent the missionaries, and that their fellow Christians in the homeland were giving their money to pay the missionaries' expenses.

When the end of the month came, the workers were paid and told that when God sent enough money, they would be called back to work. The men drew aside and talked quietly to one another for a few minutes. Then they returned and their spokesman said, "We are not going to leave you, we are going to work. We don't need the money. We will work for you for nothing."

"No, no! We would not want you to do that."

"It does not matter. We are going to work for you, and if at the end of the month God has supplied your needs, then you can pay us. If not, you do not owe us a penny."

With only one exception all the workmen said the same thing and returned to their jobs.

This action of the workmen seemed to be a turning point and the beginning of their interest in the message. Every morning at prayer-time they would pray that God would supply the needs. The days of the month passed, and finally the mail

Above and Below: several Wallamo young men worked for the missionaries at Soddo. Davis

Right, a friendly Wallamo girl smiles for the camera. Davis

The first mail delivered to the pioneer party in Soddo took six weeks to reach them via these mail carriers. SIM

Wallamo men harvest grain with oxen. **SIM**

Tools of harvest. **SIM—H. Atkins**

Wallamo women and girls draw the water. This young girl wears the apron of string and beads appropriate for her unmarried state. **Füssle** came. Mail in those days was carried on the postman's head from Addis Ababa, two hundred fifty miles or more up and down the mountain trails. Since it usually required at least seven days' walking to get to Soddo, mails were infrequent. This mail contained a letter from a friend of Mrs. Lewis, a woman who had taught her in primary school. In the letter was a $5 bill. Exchanged into Ethiopian money through the Indian traders in Soddo, there was sufficient to pay the wages of all who worked — with some left over!

This incident made a deep impression upon the Wallamo workmen, who ranged in age from 8 to 25. It was their first opportunity to see God working in answer to prayer. After this their interest in the missionaries' activities increased, and they paid closer attention to their teaching.

But as the younger men began to listen more and more eagerly to the Gospel, the old men openly ridiculed them saying, "This nonsense we do not believe, and you will not see any of the older men following in this new way."

About this time the Lewis' first baby was born — a boy. Africans love children, and their coming into the home is always interpreted as a favorable omen of the blessing of God. People from everywhere came to greet the Lewises and to rejoice with them over their son. The rejoicing was soon turned into mourning, however. The baby died on the third day. People continued to come in great numbers, but to offer their sympathy and consolation, according to Wallamo custom.

In the early morning, as the tiny grave was dug beside the mission house, the whole station compound was filled with people. The Lewises' sorrow was mingled with joy for they saw among the mourners many who had actively opposed the Gospel. The Wallamos have a custom that one must attend the funeral service of even his worst enemy, or else he will be linked with the witchcraft that may have caused death. So their coming was due mainly to fear rather than to respect and concern for the Lewises.

Among those who came to the funeral was the Governor of Wallamo with his retinue of several hundred courtiers and soldiers. As the Governor reached the edge of the mission compound, he dismounted from his mule and walked up to the gate, hat in hand. Shaking hands with Mr. Lewis, he put his other arm around him, quoting from the Scriptures: "David said, 'I shall go to him, but he shall not return to me.'" He came into the house and spoke comforting words to Mrs. Lewis. (An Amhara and an Orthodox Copt he was somewhat familiar with the Bible.) His visit made a great impression upon the people.

Large crowds continued to come to Otona for seven days after the funeral, giving the missionaries a chance to talk about Jesus Christ to people from great distances and every section of the Wallamo district. What was humanly a cause for sorrow God used as an opening wedge of interest into many hearts.

Not long after the funeral, tragedy struck a family group one night not far from the mission station. Slave-raiders dug a tunnel under the wall and through the earthen floor of the one-room house. Generally Africans sleep very soundly, so the intruders were able to work undetected. When the occupants of the house did awake, they raised the alarm, but two men and one woman were murdered. The dead woman was the mother of several children, the youngest of whom was under two. The older children were taken to the homes of relatives, but the little boy was too small to be of any use to anyone — too small to herd cows or follow the goats. Besides, he was infested with tapeworms and always hungry. As a result, he did not get much attention.

As she slowly regained her strength, Mrs. Lewis visited in the homes of the people nearby. In one of them she found this little neglected boy, Asala. Still suffering from the loss of her first child, she was quick to notice and respond to little children. As she saw Asala her heart went out to him and she said, "If I had a little boy like that, I would take good care of him."

A few weeks later Mr. Lewis met Asala's sister coming up the path from the stream with a water-pot on her back. After greeting him, she said, "You know, we are going to give you Asala."

"I did not think much about it at the moment," said Mr. Lewis afterwards, "for often the people say things like this they really do not mean." But a few days later, on a cold, rainy morning, the girl came with Asala accompanied by the relatives. They all came into the house and sat down on the living room floor where Mrs. Lewis served them something to eat. Suddenly all talk ceased, the group stood up and abruptly took their leave, saying, "We have given you Asala."

When the Lewis' cook, Walde, heard this he was greatly agitated. "What are you going to do?" he exclaimed.

"Well," said Mr. Lewis, "it looks like they have given us their little boy."

"But they can't do that!"

"It seems they have already done it."

Walde grew very excited. "But the people all know that the boy is going to die. When he dies the witch doctor will say that you have killed him. Then the people will all believe him when he says that it is your purpose in coming here to steal our little children, to eat them, and to send their blood and their spirits to your country. You cannot take him."

However, there was nothing that the Lewises could do but give their very best care to the little chap and trust God to keep him alive. They prayed daily that God would save his life and enable him to grow up, and would turn this seeming threat to the work into a blessing.

Tenderly caring for little Yohanna (John), as they now called him, they bathed him, clothed him, and sought to relieve him of the jiggers and tapeworm. Slowly through the months, with many ups and downs, Yohanna began to assume the attitudes of a normal little boy. His Wallamo name, Asala, meant happiness, but there had been no happiness in his life, until God provided a place for him in the Lewis home.

As they watched the people's reaction to the Gospel in the days following the coming of Yohanna to their home, the Lewises could certainly say with Paul, " . . . the things which happened unto me" — the death of one son, the care of an orphan boy — "have fallen out rather unto the furtherance of the gospel." Many Wallamos showed an open concern for the message of Jesus Christ.

PART III
"I WILL BUILD MY CHURCH"

Biru   Füssle

Wandaro   Füssle

*Biru and
his family.
He was a great
help to the
first missionaries.*
SIM—
Mrs. Guy Playfair

*Wandaro and
his children.
When he first
heard the Gospel
"it was like honey
to my stomach,"
he said.* SIM

5.—·Foundation Stones

. . . look unto the rock whence ye are hewn, and to
the hole of the pit whence you are digged.

— Isaiah 51:1

"WHEN THE BABY IS BORN, bury it! When I return I do not want to find it here. Slaves enough! Children enough! Listen carefully to what I say! Do away with it!"

With these parting instructions to his most trusted slave, the wealthy slave owner left his village in the Wallamo-speaking area of Kulu, across the great Omo River Canyon from Soddo, and was gone for several months. Why he did not want children is not known. But he did not. And if a Wallamo wanted no family, he would bury the babies alive as they were born.

The baby was born soon after his father left, and his mother named him Biru (Silver). Though she feared the child's father, she loved the baby more, and she would not let the slave touch Biru. And as the baby grew, so did her love.

In the village there was great apprehension and fear. What would the father do when he returned and found the baby alive? He might perhaps be angry enough to kill more than just the child.

God's purposes, however, required that Biru be spared. For although these events were taking place some time during the first decade of this century, long before the first missionaries came to the Wallamo district, God was planning for His church. The foundation stones of the Wallamo church were dug from vastly different quarries and presented widely differing personalities. Biru was to be one of them.

The time came for Biru's father to return. As he neared the village, the slaves went out to meet him and to report to him what had happened. They told of all that had taken place, the condition of the farms, the crops and the cattle. Then the father asked, "What about the baby?" They replied fearfully, "The baby is alive; his mother would not let us bury him. He is alive and growing." Furious at the news, the father ordered his head slave to go and get the baby.

But some of the women of the village had anticipated this order. One of them snatched the child and ran with him through a banana patch to the home of his uncle, an influential man in the tribe in that area. When Biru's uncle heard the story, he went to the local chief and got an order countermanding the action of the father, who was at that moment on his way to prepare the grave to bury his child. The father was placed under a curse by the chief if he would dare to harm Biru. Because of his superstition and fear of the power of the curse, the man was afraid to take the life of his son.

Although he could not now kill him, he treated Biru more cruelly than a slave. Biru grew up fearing his father, hating almost everything and everyone around him. At the age of twelve or thirteen he ran away from home, and eventually wandered to Addis Ababa. There he came in contact with the Swedish Mission where he heard the Gospel and accepted Christ as his Saviour. Entering the Swedish Mission School he learned to read Amharic and showed great interest in the Word of God.

When the original party of the S.I.M. were preparing to enter the interior in 1928, Biru, now about twenty, learned of their plan and made himself known to them. They agreed to take him on as an employee. So, after many years, he found himself again in Wallamo country. In the early days of the work and especially because of his helpful though meager knowledge of English, he was of great assistance in many ways. His contact and work was principally with Walter Ohman, through whose influence the Lord was able to work in Biru's life. His experience of salvation and his faith in Christ were deepened. In many ways God was preparing Biru to be a strong leader in the future church.

One day early in the experience of the missionaries at Soddo, Selma Bergsten observed a young lad standing by the fence, a troubled look on his face. It was Godana, one of several boys who had heard the Gospel while working for the Mission, and had given their lives to Jesus Christ.

Godana's concern was simply that when work was over that day he had no place to spend the night. His father was dead and he lived with his mother. But the night before when he returned home, he found the door firmly closed. He tried to open it but it was securely tied.

From inside the grass hut, Godana's mother answered his call. "You cannot stay here any longer. You may not sleep here. We will not have any of this Jesus matter in this house. I have tied your lamb behind the house. Take him with you wherever you go."

"Where did you and the lamb go?" asked Miss Bergsten. Godana told her that he had taken it to his uncle's place. The uncle had kept him overnight, but now Godana was troubled. Where would he and the lamb go tonight? It was not so much

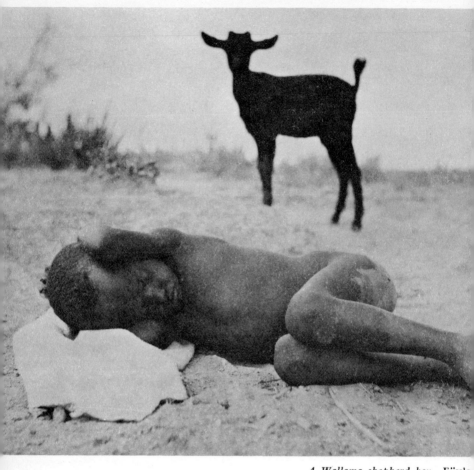

A Wallamo shepherd boy. Füssle

that he himself must leave home; he was deeply concerned that his little lamb had to leave.

"You may leave early from work today, in order to find a place where you and the lamb can stay," Miss Bergsten told him.

When Godana left work that day he took his lamb back to his uncle's home. His uncle had heard the Gospel previously and was a believer. He was willing to let Godana and his lamb make their home with him. In this action, too, God was preparing the foundation stones of the Wallamo Church.

Wandaro was living proof of the wisdom of God. Men would have passed him by, for he had none of the outward marks of leadership. "Man," however, "looketh on the outward appearance, but God looketh upon the heart." God saw the precious jewel; men could only see the rough stone. How wrong men would have been. Wandaro's own testimony reveals his worth.

"I was on my way to Sunday market," he relates. "It was a cold, wet day and I had left home before daylight. Traveling along I neared Otona, where the road passes through the white man's village. There he was standing beside a strange looking building. He called to me to come. I saw other Wallamos standing near by, so I thought it was quite safe to go.

"It was raining quite hard and very wet outside, so I and the others were invited to enter a small grass-roofed building. It smelled strangely in there because of the medicine the white people kept in that building to give to sick people who came to them for help. We sat on the floor, and the white man sat there too in the middle of us. He was a very young man, he had no beard, his face and hands were very pale, his clothes were strange. He didn't speak our language very well, but I listened and I liked what he said. When he invited us to return again after seven days, I determined to go.

"I was there and listened once more to what the white man

had to say. He was talking about a person called Jesus. This person was sent by God into the world. He did many wonderful things. The white man had a book in his hand, and he told us that God had given them this book. God said in the book that any man, even a Wallamo, who wanted forgiveness for his sin and peace in his heart, could have it if he would become a follower of Jesus. Somehow this just seemed like honey to my stomach, and so I thought I must come again and hear more.

"Seven days passed and I was again at Otona. The white man told us over and over again that there were many bad things we had done and this greatly displeased God. We should believe in Jesus and He would forgive us and take our sin away. He spoke directly to me and asked if I wanted to believe. I told him that my father was a witch doctor. He was the spiritual leader of all the people who lived near him on Mount Humbo."

After hearing the Gospel for the third time, Wandaro opened his heart and gave himself to Jesus Christ. Immediately his life was changed. For one thing he had a great desire to learn to read. But the Bible was available only in Amharic, the language of the ruling class which was, for the most part, quite unknown to the average Wallamo person.

The Amharic language, which remotely resembles Hebrew, is composed of 33 different consonant sounds with seven vowel forms of each. In addition to this, there are numerous diphthongs, which bring the total number of characters in its alphabet to 256. This is quite a task for even a well-educated person to master, and Wandaro was certainly not this. In fact, he was probably slower than average in ability. However, when reading classes were conducted, Wandaro walked from his village fifteen miles away to attend these classes several times a week.

Mrs. Lewis had taught several of the young Christians to read. She met her match in Wandaro, however, for somehow he seemed utterly unable to comprehend. He just could not grasp the Amharic alphabet. He soon fell behind the others in the group and became quite discouraged. Then Mrs. Lewis became ill and was confined to her room for long periods at a time. Concern for Wandaro prompted her to offer him special lessons three times a week. Often she would notice him, head bowed in prayer, asking the Lord for help to learn just one more letter. After a period of study when he had been able to comprehend the lesson, he would bow his head in a prayer of thanksgiving. This might occur several times each lesson. If he mastered one letter of the alphabet each day he was satisfied.

With Mrs. Lewis' patient help, Wandaro did learn to read Amharic fairly well — though never fluently.

One day Wandaro stood up in a Sunday morning service and asked permission to speak. He pointed out that the crowds of people who were coming to hear the Gospel far exceeded the capacity of the small clinic building on the Mission station in which the meetings were held. He suggested that just as they built their own homes by helping one another, so the people should build a house in which to worship God.

The proposal was welcomed by the believers. During the day they worked on their farms and in the late afternoon and evening hours they built the meeting house at the edge of the mission station. The building was made of mud blocks, like some of the other station buildings. The missionaries helped too, working with their hands often by the light of lanterns. This made a great impression upon the people. Around nine o'clock each night some of the Wallamo women brought prepared parched corn and coffee. After this a Bible study course was conducted before the people went home.

One evening as they sat around a fire, sharing their humble fare, Wandaro told more about his conversion and the results of it. "I tell you, honestly, although I didn't understand much about what I was doing at that time, and I do not fully understand it even yet, when I stood up and with my stomach stated that I wanted to believe God and follow this Jesus, something happened to me. Since that time until this very hour, my heart has been filled with joy. There is a strange peace in my stomach that I have never known before.

"After that day others too believed. Many people by that time were walking with me from Humbo to Soddo every seven days. So the white man said that if we wanted him to do so he would be willing to come out to where we lived and stay with us for a while to tell us more about Jesus.

"Just about that time my baby boy, two rainy seasons old, became ill. My father, who is the witch doctor, said my baby's sickness was because I had rejected my father's religion. I had turned away from our family gods and followed this new God called Jesus. He said that unless I again returned to the worship of our family clan and offered sacrifices to the demons, the sick baby would surely die. This was known throughout all our villages nearby. But a voice within me said I should not return to the worship of our ancestors and demons and Satan himself. So I said, 'No, I will not sacrifice to the demons again. No matter what happens to me or my child, I will not do it.'

"After a little while the baby died. At the funeral (you know our custom) all the people came to weep, to wail, to scratch and cut their faces and chests most terribly. I asked them not to do it. I told them that they should stop, they should not weep, for my own heart was not bitter or sad. Yes, it was true that I felt the death of my child was a great loss, but I had a strange sense of peace and well-being in my stomach and I did not want them to weep.

"My wife was just a young girl. She was so bound up with the rites of paganism and demons, that she persisted in wailing and cutting her face and doing all sorts of things, even cursing God. I told her that she should not do this. She became very angry with me. After seven days of mourning were finished, she told me she was leaving and returning to her parents. She said she could not live with anyone who had such little love for his family not to offer a sacrifice to his father's gods in order to save his own child's life. So she left.

"I found out then, as I have found many times since, that this message the white man reads from the Book of God is true. Though I am just a simple Wallamo and not very learned in the ways of the world, no one can tell me that these words from the book and my following Jesus do not produce peace in my stomach. I know in my stomach that God has forgiven me my sin and that I am His child."

Wandaro's wife later returned to him, largely as a result of Wandaro's changed life. His kind and loving manner was so different from the Wandaro she had known in the past. She listened to Wandaro and believed the message he constantly told to one and all he met. Together they served the Lord faithfully for many years.

6 ~ Jesus Christ vs. Satan

To open their eyes, and to turn them from darkness to light, and from the power of Satan unto God . . .
— Acts 26:18

Born and brought up in a pagan village, Diasa was trained in the many and varied arts of witchcraft. Later he came in contact with Muslims and sought to follow as best he knew how the teaching of that religion.

By the time he met the missionaries he was about fifty years old and had tried every form of religion known to him. But he was still a miserable man reaching out for the tiniest straw of hope that would meet the great oppressing need of his heart. He came frequently to listen to the words about a salvation through faith in Jesus Christ.

Finally, after many hearings, Diasa uncertainly, almost fearfully, professed faith in Christ. There was no instantaneous change in his life. Because of his rather unstable nature, he found it particularly difficult to turn his back on the other religions he had known and trust solely in Christ.

Even though he was by this time a grown man with some gray hairs, Diasa had a great desire to learn to read. So he

60

attended the day school on the station, along with the fourteen-
and fifteen-year-old boys. Because he spoke Amharic fluently
it was less of a problem for him to learn to read than for
Wandaro, for instance, and he made good progress.

Reading the Bible changed Diasa's whole life; instead of a
hesitant, fearful Christian he became a wholehearted, courageous man. He asked to have his name changed from Darge, by
which he had been known up to this time, to Diasa. "I do not
want to be called Darge any more," he said. "This is the name
I had when I worshiped Satan. This is the name I was known
by as a witch doctor, and I no longer want to be known in
that way. I want to take the name that my father first gave
me, Diasa."

Diasa was so filled with love for Jesus Christ that he wanted
to speak about Him everywhere. Even though he was the night
watchman, and therefore supposed to keep awake, he would
take cat naps and get some rest during the night. During the
day, then, he had plenty of time to talk to people. The numerous Wallamo funerals gave him ample opportunity to speak
of Jesus Christ to the crowds of people who came to pay their
respects to the dead and to offer sympathy to those that
mourned. Diasa would sit down with the people, talking to
them quietly about the future life.

One morning the death wail sounded across the deep canyon
that separated the mission station at Otona from the next hill-
side. A wealthy Wallamo had died. One could see his house,
surrounded by garden and trees, from Otona. Diasa had crossed
the valley many times to witness to this man, but he had been
too proud to listen. Now he was dead, gone into eternity
without Christ.

Knowing that all the great witch doctors of the area would
attend the funeral, along with hundreds of other people, Diasa
crossed the valley early the morning of the funeral. Before

sitting down he paid his respects to those who mourned, sympathizing with them. But he did not follow the ordinary Wallamo custom. The others marched up and down in front of the mourners, turning somersaults, scratching themselves with their long finger nails and beating their chests. Taking little bundles of sharp thorns they slashed their cheeks until the blood ran streaming down their faces and over their bodies. By this convulsive effort they hoped to show the depth of their sense of loss and the sincerity of their sympathy.

Diasa, by contrast, walked quietly and sympathetically among the relatives, quoting the words of Jesus: "Let not your heart be troubled, believe in God, believe also in me. In my Father's house are many mansions. If it were not so, I would have told you." He assured them that though it was too late for the man who had died, it was not too late for those who remained and mourned his death. They still had an opportunity to believe in Jesus Christ. Then he went off and sat down under a tree with the rest of the crowd, where he continued to witness to them.

While he was sitting there, he noticed the chief of all the witch doctors in Wallamo seated not far from him. This witch doctor was a peculiar looking fellow with seven bunches of long hair on his head, braided in seven parts. Everybody in the entire Wallamo tribe feared him greatly. He was believed to have killed hundreds of people through the curses and hexes he put on them. His compound was a great enclosure. Passing through the door of the first enclosure, one entered a second enclosure, then a third. No one but the witch doctor himself could enter the third enclosure — a narrow circle around the house where the witch doctor went to meet the devil when he wanted to call upon the spirits. This enclosure was surrounded by a fence made of spears, and every spear had come from a man whom he had cursed. When a man died upon whom he had pronounced a curse, the relatives were duty bound to give the dead man's spear to the witch doctor. It was no wonder that everyone feared him and trembled in his presence.

Diasa, however, was not afraid. He continued to tell the people that it was not necessary to weep as they were doing. He told them of Jesus Christ and His power to set men free from the power of Satan. The people grew restless, fearing that this teaching would not please the witch doctor, and they began to try to silence Diasa.

"Be careful," they said. "Watch out. Don't say that any more."

But Diasa would not be quieted and talked louder and louder.

Finally the witch doctor spoke. "Shut up!" he commanded.

"Who are you to tell me to shut up?" Diasa replied.

The people were terrified at Diasa's boldness, so fearful were they of this man. They did not want Diasa to be killed by his curse. "Be quiet," they urged again. "Don't say anymore."

But Diasa would not be stilled. "Who are you to tell me to be quiet?" he continued to the witch doctor. "The Lord Jesus Christ, the Son of God, told me to tell people this message everywhere, and no man can tell me to shut up. The Lord has told me to tell it."

Then the witch doctor became very angry. "Do you not know who I am?"

"Yes, I know who you are," Diasa said. "I know you are a witch doctor, and I know that you do not know Jesus Christ as your Saviour."

"Do you not fear Gotcha Godo (chief of the witch doctors)?"

"No, I do not fear. I revere Jesus Christ. You are the one who is causing the people to be bound in fear, who is giving them so much trouble. Jesus Christ is able to save. He can break your power, and He can give life and light and liberty to the people when they believe on Him."

The bold words of Diasa enraged Gotcha Godo. "Before six months are up," he shouted, "before the next *meskal** comes, one of the white men's servants is going to die!"

"There are many people that follow the white man's teaching. Even so, it is not the white man's teaching, but God's teaching, and there are many of us here who follow God. It is quite possible that some one of them would die during the next six months. Now if you mean me, why don't you call me by name?" Diasa spoke calmly.

Gotcha Godo became even more furious. Looking directly at Diasa, he extended his thin bony hand and put the long fingernail of his fore-finger down on the ground, pointing the other fingers at Diasa. His voice rasped as he spat out the words.

"Before six months are up, before the next *meskal* season comes around, *you* will be dead!"

There was a heavy silence as the people who heard the curse pronounced scarcely dared to breathe. They drew back and watched in wide-eyed wonder, expecting something evil and violent to happen to Diasa immediately.

Turning to the people and lifting up his arms to prevent any uproar, Diasa spoke. "You have heard what this wicked man has said. He is a liar, and his father is the devil, who is the father of lies. Now you who have heard this, I want you to watch. If his evil curse upon me works, if I am dead before the next *meskal* comes, six months from now, then go ahead and worship the devil and follow him. But if I am alive, I want you to turn to Jesus Christ, accept Him as your Saviour, and come and worship God with me!"

What Diasa had said and done had never happened before. He had not only challenged the chief witch doctor of the Wallamo people, but, in fact, the devil himself. There can be no

*The big celebration of witchcraft at which they were to offer the "sacrifice" celebration to Satan, was just six months away.

doubt that he had been given courage and empowered by the Holy Spirit that day.

Yet even an Elijah experienced fear. That evening a trembling Diasa came to Mr. Lewis, before he went to work, to tell what he had done.

"Teacher, did I do right?"

Mr. Lewis replied, "Yes, you did right, but you have to remember now that you have challenged Satan. But do not be afraid. The Lord Jesus Christ is more powerful than Satan. Christ Himself has said, 'Be of good cheer; I have overcome the world.' He has said, 'All power in heaven and earth is given unto me.' He is the All-Powerful One, and He is the One who has power over Satan. You know, Diasa, since you are a believer and have trusted your soul to Christ, He will protect you. The devil cannot curse you." Together they read in the Word of God the promises of assurance and of God's abiding presence, and Diasa was strengthened.

"Let us pray about it and commit the matter entirely to God. You must be very careful where you go, where you eat. This witch doctor and all those who support him are going to try in every way possible to bring about the fulfillment of this curse he has pronounced upon you. If you sit down to eat somewhere, somebody might try to poison you. Therefore be very careful for these next six months, where you go, where you eat, and how you conduct yourself."

Evening by evening as Diasa came to work they prayed together. God gave him strength and courage so that he was relieved from his fear and his heart was filled with peace. Only a person who has himself experienced the bondage of Satan's slavery and has been freed from it can fully appreciate what it meant to Diasa and the other believers to have challenged the hosts of wickedness — and now to be experiencing deliverance from Satan's awful power.

At the end of six months the time for the *meskal* celebration arrived. It was held out on the broad plains six or seven miles from the mission station near the home of Gotcha Godo, the great witch doctor. People gathered that day by the thousands. Mr. Lewis describes what took place:

"Diasa mounted one of my horses. Desita, another of the believers, rode one, and I joined them. We crossed the valley to the witch doctor's place. The plains were filled with horsemen, six hundred or more, playing games and throwing spears at each other. We approached the place where the witch doctor sat, and there were the devil dancers. The seven devil drums were being beaten incessantly. A huge tree, a particular species used only for this purpose, had been cut down. The branches were left intact, and it was set in the ground so as to appear it was growing there. Little bunches of grass were tied to its branches. The people were dancing to the beating of the drums.

"Then suddenly the drums changed beat. It was time for the people to assemble. They gathered in closely for the sacrifice of the great Passover celebration to Satan. In the midst of this place with hundreds and hundreds of people gathered round, we stood near the old witch doctor himself. The drummers again changed their rhythmic beat — the dance took on a more portentous, ominous note. The people began to sing in the worship of Satan as preparation was made to offer the sacrifice.

"Diasa sprang to his feet and addressed himself to the witch doctor. He said, 'Gotcha Godo, do you remember me? I am the one you said would not be living on this day. I want to testify that your god has no power, that the devil is a liar, and that you are a liar! I am here, and I am in good health! You said I would not live to the time of the *meskal*, but here I am!

" 'Now,' said Diasa, turning to the people, 'you remember what I said? I said, if I am dead, then go and serve Satan, but if I am alive, then turn to God. There were many of you there

Wallamo men listen questioningly to the Gospel for the first time. Davis

A Wallamo witch doctor uses his smoke pot. His drum is between his feet. SIM

Musicians and dancers set the tempo. Füssle

that day who said you would do just this. Now here I am, well and alive. I want you to turn to Jesus Christ and accept Him as your Saviour.'

"It was still as death. All eyes were riveted upon the witch doctor. No one dared to move or speak. Never before in living memory had anyone dared to challenge the life-and-death power of this priest of Satan. Fear was etched deeply upon their faces. What awful thing would happen now? Surely Diasa would be struck dead on the spot. They dared not touch him. Those nearby drew back in cringing unbelief — it could not be that any man could defy the Gotcha Godo and live.

"The drumming ceased and the dancers stood motionless. The witch doctor glared in anger at Diasa. The silence was almost unbearable. Diasa and his companion stood alone, singled out from the crowd. The agent of Satan and the child of God faced each other for what seemed an interminable interval. Bewilderment wreathed the witch doctor's face and his hands fell weakly at his side. He turned and like a whipped animal retreated to his enclosure.

"Pandemonium now broke loose as the spell was broken and people fled from the place in terror. That was the end of the witch doctor's meeting, and his powerful hold on the people was broken."

7 ～ The First Church

> ... *conformed to the image of his Son, that* [*they*]
> *might be the firstborn among many brethren.*
>
> — Romans 8:29

"WE HAVEN'T DONE EVERYTHING YET! We haven't done everything yet!" Desita came excitedly up to Earl Lewis holding his Bible.

"What's the matter, Desita?"

" 'They believed and were *baptized!*' I read it here that they believed and were baptized. So we haven't done everything yet."

Desita was one of several Wallamo young men working at Otona for the missionaries. He and Walde, the Lewis' cook, were among the first to take a definite stand for Jesus Christ. But when he did, his young wife left him. One of her reasons was that because he accepted the white man's religion, he stopped beating her, and the other women taunted her — "Your husband is just a weak woman; he is not a man." Nothing that Desita said could change his wife's mind. "I will never come back," she said.

If he could have persuaded his wife to stay, Desita would probably have been caught in the witchcraft in which her

whole family was involved. His mother, too, was a strong
believer in witchcraft and made life hard for him. But because
his wife left, his Christian commitment was strengthened. A
short time later he and two other young men, professing Christians, were chosen by the Lewises to dig the grave for the Lewis
baby and to help with the burial. When he saw how Christians
reacted to sorrow and death, he determined that if he ever
married again, his wife would be a Christian.

Desita was a bright student, although he was perhaps 25
when he first learned the Amharic alphabet from Mrs. Lewis,
and he was soon able to teach others. He had worked for a
former governor of Wallamo for several years, so he knew how
to speak Amharic. He became a fluent reader of Amharic, and
his constant reading of the Scriptures made him an active
leader of the other Christians. When he read that the New
Testament believers were baptized, he suggested having a baptismal service.

So a general conference of the missionaries was called at
Soddo late in 1933, and all the believers who were interested in
being baptized were invited to attend a special meeting. Desita
was one of the 16 (out of a possible 23) who came to the
meeting, along with his new wife Mamiti — whom he had married only after being sure that she was a real Christian.

During the first part of the meeting, each believer was questioned individually about his Christian experience by all of
the missionaries, and eventually 13 were considered ready for
baptism.

Then followed a period of discussion in which the meaning
of baptism was stressed — salvation was received by faith alone,
not by doing or not doing anything; so that baptism could not
save, but it was a witness to their friends and neighbors that
they were new people and that Jesus Christ lived in them.

Finally Desita stood and faced the Wallamo believers.

"We can lie to deceive the white man, but few of us can fool one another and none of us can fool God. Some of us have quit smoking the pipe, but we continue to raise tobacco and sell it to others. Some of us have already stopped drinking beer, but we make it and sell it in the market place, or our wives sell it. Are we going to lie to God?

"God knows our hearts, and both He and we know whether these old things have passed out of our lives or not."

Then he turned to the missionaries.

"You have examined us. Do you have any objection if we examine ourselves?"

"No, of course not," the missionaries replied.

Desita turned to the story of Annanias and Sapphira and read it to the group. When they learned how the judgment of God came upon those who claimed to be followers of Jesus, they were deeply impressed. During the questioning that followed, the underlying concern of the Christians proved to be the matter of circumcision.

In the cutural and social customs of the Wallamos, circumcision was more than a physical hygenic measure. It was the most important part of the initiation ceremony whereby a boy was recognized as mature and ready to assume the status of a full-fledged male member of the tribe. Its religious significance was indicated by the fact that no uncircumcised male was permitted to participate in or partake of a sacrifice to the spirits.

Because of its cultural implications, the believers agreed to require of every candidate for baptism that he promise not to submit to circumcision for any purpose related to the ancient Wallamo custom.* This careful and strict self-discipline resulted in the elimination of three more Christians from the

*This has continued to be a requirement for every baptismal candidate, both men and women, since initiation ceremonies for girls also include the rite of circumcision. A circumcised man would not take an uncircumcised girl for a wife.

*Believers met in one another's homes
as well as on the mission station. Here
they were outside Desita's house.* Davis

*Chormo and his wife
Pakarei and their chil-
dren.* Davis

*Walter Ohman
and Earl Lewis
baptized the first
converts on the
mission station.* SIM

baptismal candidates, leaving only ten. On December 10, 1933, the first ten Wallamos were baptized in a large pit on the mission compound, just five and a half years after the first missionaries came. There were eight men and two women: Desita and his wife Mamiti; Chormo and his wife Pakarei; Diasa, Araybo, Biru, Wandaro, Godana, and Cowna Cubba.

Two weeks later the first Communion service was held for the believers. Familiar Wallamo foods were used for the elements — cornbread and honey mixed with water. During the service Mamiti said, "I never realized how much God loved us until we looked at the broken bread and saw that these little pieces of broken bread showed how much Christ suffered for us, because He was broken for us."

Desita's reaction to taking Communion was that God demanded holiness. "A follower of Christ will not ask someone to eat food that he would not eat himself, thinking, 'It is not fit to eat.' "

"Does this mean food alone?" someone asked.

"No, no! But it means anything that you should not do as a Christian you would not ask someone else to do.

"The way to God is a narrow way, but it is broad enough to receive the greatest sinner who will come and confess his sin, and it is narrow enough that the sinner cannot get through unless he has put away sin."

After their baptism, the eight men took turns preaching in the regular services of the church. Soon they decided to choose three elders to take the responsibility for the group. By the time of the second baptismal services, Desita, Diasa and Godana had been elected elders, and they conducted both the examinations and the baptisms.

The next two years were a time of advance. The Bible classes met four nights a week. On Saturday night a missionary would give a special message to be used by the Wallamos on Sunday in their preaching around the countryside. In the Sunday night services they would report on their experiences and tell how the Lord had blessed them during the previous week.

Several other mission stations in Wallamo territory were started, too — at Gofa first, to the southwest, then at Gamo near Lake Abaya. The missionary force was increased. And slowly the number of Christians grew.

The elders elected by the Wallamo Christians held the second baptismal service at Soddo in 1935. **Davis**

8.—Christianity and Culture

. . . a new creature: old things are passed away;
behold, all things are become new.
— II Corinthians 5:17

"NO BEER, NO BUILDING!"

Angry voices resounded through the clear morning air. "No beer, no building! We will not help you build if you do not give us beer!"

But no beer was forthcoming — only coffee and food. Slowly the large group dwindled, as one by one the Wallamo men returned to their own homes. Finally only a handful were left — a disturbed Diasa who had hoped to begin work on a new house that day, and a few Christian friends who had helped prepare the food and coffee.

Life in Wallamo, from time immemorial, was a communal affair. Everything conformed to the cultural pattern. The plowing of new ground, the building of a house, the celebration of a birth, the burying of the dead — these things were done together. And usually they were accompanied by the consumption of great quantities of beer.

When a man wanted to build a new house, for instance, all he had to do was to announce the day upon which he planned to begin work, and his friends and neighbors from near and far would come to help. Often they would bring with them bundles of grass or poles as their personal contribution to the effort. They were rewarded by the provision of beer to drink, and in turn, of course, were helped in the building of their own homes as the occasion arose.

The Wallamo Christians found that their new way of life and new loyalty to Jesus Christ cut diametrically across the old tribal manner of life. Since the Christians had given up the drinking and preparation of intoxicating liquor, Diasa did not serve beer at his house-building bee. But when his neighbors and friends discovered the lack, even the copious quantities of good food and coffee did not change their minds. They refused to work and returned to their homes.

Faced with this new and difficult problem for which they had no precedent, the *believers and missionaries conferred together, and asked God for His direction and guidance. Eventually they agreed that they should stand by their decision not to provide beer, even though this had been the custom, since it was inconsistent with their Christian testimony. And they resolved to help each other in the building of their homes. As a result, even the missionaries joined heartily in the building, performing tasks that were strange and unfamiliar.

For several days all the Christians worked on the new house. The unbelieving neighbors and friends were perplexed as they watched, but also greatly impressed by the steadfastness and sincerity of the new Christians. One by one, they began to return to help with the work, until there were a sufficient number of workmen to complete the job satisfactorily.

This radical break with the old way of life, coming at the

beginning of the church in the Wallamo area, effectively set the pattern to follow. It did not come at the white man's instigation, but arose naturally from the confrontation of Christianity and Wallamo culture. And the discipline of standing by principle strengthened the young believers.

At the same time, however, it created great embarrassment, considerable difficulty, and was often misunderstood — even between friends. In some cases, old friends who had not believed were willing to help build without the rewarding provision of drink. But many others refused. They said that any house built without beer would not be successful. The people would not be free from the outraged ancestral spirits who had been shown such disrespect by the omission of ancient Wallamo customs.

From the very first, Christianity became a natural thing to the Wallamo Christians, and they did not consider it as something introduced from the outside. This was what the missionaries hoped for — they wanted to leave as much of the Wallamo way of life as untouched as possible. This meant trying not to introduce Western cultural patterns into the Wallamo church, patterns which were really extraneous to essential Christianity.

So it was the natural thing for the Wallamos to build their churches like their own houses. Although the first building put up on the mission station for church meetings was made of mud blocks like the other station buildings, the Christians somehow never thought of it as a church — just as a community meeting house. Their own homes were circular, and made of logs and branches. A two-foot circular trench is dug with the proper diameter, in which fairly large logs are stood upright. These are firmly bound together, starting at the bottom with rope and purlins made of small pliable branches wound together. There is just one door and no windows.

Orthodox Coptic church buildings have quite a different style of architecture.
Davis

Sakala (p. 164) built this new grass hut for the missionaries' visit.
Davis

A congregation near Soddo meets outside their own church building made in the style of their houses. SIM — B. Adams

The first churches were not built until after the missionaries left, and on a larger scale than a home, with several doors for better ventilation. *Wosa Kayta,* they are called — "house of prayer."

Wallamo meetings require no furniture, and none was ever used when the believers met on the mission station. The people would sit down on the floor, not in rows, but wherever there was space, so that a large number of people could be crowded into a small area. As a rule men sat in one section, women in another. The speaker or preacher never used a pulpit.

At least once the Wallamos *rejected* Western ways for their own — in the matter of church music. Western tunes and the words of Western hymns translated by the missionaries somehow could not be adapted to Wallamo ears and sense of rhythm. They just didn't understand or appreciate them. Little by little the Wallamo Christians began to compose their own songs.

Wallamo singing is a chant which repeats two notes and the same musical interval again and again. It is always antiphonal. People sing while they work together, travel together — any occasion seems to be good for a song. A leader sings a phrase followed by the rest of the people chanting a refrain in unison.

This was the form of music that the Wallamos understood, that expressed their feelings more adequately. The words and rhythms came naturally out of their own experiences, their love for Jesus Christ, their understanding of the Christian life. New hymns, or at least new lines for hymns could often be composed on the spot by a song leader completely involved in the singing.

One of the favorite hymns was "God is the Word of life." The leader sings, "God is the Word of life." *"God is the Word of life,"* repeats the congregation.

> God gives the Word of Life,   (Leader)
> *God is the Word of Life.*   (Refrain)

God gives the yoke that is light, (Leader)
 God is the Word of Life. (Refrain)
God gives to men and women,
 God is the Word of Life.
God gives us joy and peace,
 God is the Word of Life.
God is no respector of persons,
 God is the Word of Life.

"We will rise," was composed for singing at Christian funerals.

When the Lord calls us from the grave, (Leader)
 We will rise. (Refrain)
When He comes for His own,
 We will rise.
Those who have gone before will rise,
 We will rise.
He will raise us from the grave,
 We will rise.
He will come when we least expect Him.
 We will rise.

Then the refrain changes:

The one who has just left us,
 He will rise. (or *She will rise.*)
The grave will not hold him,
 He will rise.
We will meet him again . . .
We will meet where no sickness enters . . .
We will meet where no pains are known . . .
We will meet where no taxes trouble . . .
We will meet him where we never hunger . . .
We will meet him where we will have new clothes . . .
We will meet — we will meet,
 We will rise.
We will meet in Jesus' house,
 We will rise.
We will always live in Jesus' house,
 We will rise.

PART IV
THE FIRES OF WAR

9 ᵕ War Arrives

Ye shall not need to fight in this battle . . . .
— II Chronicles 20:17

"YOU AND MR. OHMAN are the Italians —" The Governor, Dejazmatch Ababa, turned to me. "Mr. Forsberg and I are the Amharas."

We were comfortably seated around the carrom board in the Forsbergs' home in Gofa, after a delicious dinner. But Dejazmatch Ababa's half-humorous remark was a disquieting reminder that his visit was not purely a social one. It made us remember the hundreds of Gofa soldiers bivouacked for the night in the valley just below the mission station. And though the game we played was interesting enough, the Governor's lion and leopard cubs — five of them — that romped and scampered around the table and sniffed at our legs also kept our minds on the threat of danger.

It was the first week of October, 1935. I had been in Ethiopia less than a year, and Walter and Marcella Ohman and I were on a prospecting trip, looking for new mission station sites. We were traveling by mule caravan through the high mountain ranges of southwestern Ethiopia. It was a week's

83

journey between the stations at Gamo and Gofa, and we hoped
to find some place between them to begin a new work. The
rainy season was just over, and all the rivers were full, and
waterfalls were tumbling down beside the mountain paths at
every turn. The fresh green countryside invited us to stop
everywhere. So did our knowledge that the multitudes of people
we saw had never heard of Jesus — that they needed to hear
before it was too late.

It had taken us about a week to get to Gofa from Soddo, and
for the past four or five days we had enjoyed visiting with the
Forsbergs who had been there about a year. But often we found
our conversations turning to the threats of war that were in
the air.

Throughout the late months of 1934 and the early months
of 1935, Italy had been threatening to invade Ethiopia. The
long-standing undefined border dispute over the arid desert
region between Ethiopia and Italian Somaliland was the stated
reason for the conflict. More likely, however, was the commonly
recognized desire of the Italian dictator, Il Duce Mussolini,
to create for himself an East African empire by annexing
Ethiopia.

For months Britain and France tried to negotiate with Mussolini, to find some way to appease his desire and to avoid open
conflict. Unsuccessful in their diplomatic efforts, they were
unwilling to commit their countries to come to Ethiopia's
assistance or to resist aggression. The League of Nations was
weak and vacillating — all but dead. An attack seemed imminent
and unavoidable.

The Emperor of Ethiopia, Haile Selassie I, had been busily
preparing to defend his country, alone if necessary. Yet somehow we had not believed that war would come. So the arrival
of the invasion came as a shock. Could it be? Well, here was
the army of the Governor on its way.

In the morning Dejazmatch Ababa and his troops would march off to fight the Italian invaders. In true Amharic fashion they had started out late in the day from his palace which could be seen from the Forsberg's house, and then had made camp in the valley below the mission station. (Gathering equipment together and actually getting underway is always such a job that the Amharas prefer to camp the first night only a short way from home. But at least they are started!) Many of his soldiers would never return to their homes and families in Gofa.

In other similar camps throughout Ethiopia, thousands of the Emperor's warriors were enroute to the capital and the frontiers, to defend their king and country. If raw courage and bravery were to be equated with modern military skill, the outcome of the fighting might reasonably be in doubt. However, the army of the "King of kings"* trained in modern warfare was pitifully small, and certainly no match for the might of Mussolini, his men and their machines.

Even so, it would be some time before the fighting reached down into our area, so the Ohmans and I continued on our survey trip, over to Gamo and then back to Soddo. But the loveliness of the country we were traveling through had been dimmed, and we wondered what was ahead for us and for the Wallamo church.

One year before I had come to Ethiopia in response to the challenge, issued by Dr. Bingham, for young men to open the rugged *northern* part of the country. But when I arrived in Addis Ababa on December 1, Dr. Lambie informed me that I was to go at once to Soddo to help build a hospital. Since there were threats of invasion and war, beginning work in the north

*The title "King of kings" for the Emperor of Ethiopia was taken by the present Emperor's grandfather, Menelik II, when he subdued the tribes around the Amharas and made Ethiopia a unified country under his rule.

Camp is pitched by a stream along the way. Davis

Below, Walter Ohman preaches to the Wallamo along the trail. Davis

Ray Davis. Davis

Ruth Bray with lion cubs — these belonged to the governor of Gamo. SIM

Ray Davis, Marcella Ohman, Walter Ohman traveled through Gofa on horseback in 1935. Davis

Building supplies for the hospital at Soddo came by camel caravan from Addis Ababa. Davis

The hospital was built by Ray Davis, though never completely finished because of the war. Davis

Ethiopian soldiers armed for war. Davis

seemed not too wise a move. And the fact that I had started to study architectural engineering before God's call to enter missionary work arrested me seemed to indicate that I should go south. The need for the hospital at Soddo was urgent — Dr. and Mrs. Percy Roberts and Lois Briggs were anxious to have a proper building in which to carry on their much needed medical work.

The trip to Soddo by horseback and mule caravan still took two weeks. So it was February 1st before we broke ground for the hospital outpatient and surgical section. Supplies for the construction, though, took three weeks to a month to come from the capital — by camelback — things like window and door frames, glass, nails, hardware, roofing. Stone, mud and eucalyptus trees for lumber were plentifully available in the area. I had an Indian carpenter to help me, along with willing though unskilled Wallamo workmen, and we progressed quite well, but slowly. After three months, however, funds ran out and we couldn't afford the Indian carpenter's help. And then came the war. We continued working and the hospital was eventually usable, but it never was as finished as it should have been.

When Italy invaded Ethiopia at the beginning of October, 1935, the American and British embassies advised all their citizens to leave the country immediately. They could no longer be responsible for our safety. The news was sent to Dr. Rowland Bingham, the General Director of Sudan Interior Mission, asking his advice. After a mission day of prayer, his reply came:

> You are under higher orders than those of the King of England or the President of the United States. Get your instructions from Him and we are one with with you. We approve the sending home of mothers with children.

In Ethiopia we had come to the same conclusion, and all of us decided to stay. Since we were here by God's call to bring the Gospel to these people in need, we would hardly be justified in leaving now in their hour of greatest need. We realized that staying might be dangerous, that in other circumstances God might have directed us some other way. In this instance, however, there can be no doubt, as subsequent events proved, that He led us to stay.

Addis Ababa fell May 5, 1936. The Emperor with his higher officials left the country to ask for help from the League of Nations in a futile attempt to retain Ethiopia's independence. With no central government in control, the capital was full of confusion, chaos and riot. The defeated Ethiopian soldiers began to retreat in disorder to their homes, robbing, pillaging and burning on the way in a kind of hopeless battle against despair. It became unsafe to travel on the roads.

I was packed and ready to travel north by caravan from Soddo to the capital. Let my diary tell the story:

April 29, 1936, Thursday — Shefaro arrived unexpectedly last night. He brought a letter from Clarence Duff [in Addis Ababa] advising everyone to remain as quiet as possible until the present crisis passes. Although I am not mentioned, I have decided to wait until Mr. Ohman returns in a few days to confer with him.

May 7, Thursday — We had an unexpected visit today. About 8 o'clock this morning the quiet of the countryside was disturbed as several Italian aircraft flew over the Governor's palace and the town, dropping bombs and machine gunning or strafing the streets.

May 9, Saturday — Mr. Ohman and I went into town this afternoon. We found the government post had not yet arrived. The telephone is also cut off. Rumors are rampant.

May 11, Monday — Still no mail.

May 13, Wednesday — The Sidamo mail arrived this noon with news that Dr. Roberts and Mr. Webb were returning. They arrived at 5 p.m. and brought the news of the capture of Addis Ababa by the Italians on May 5. The defeated soldiers have rioted and completely ransacked the capital; the entrance of the Italian Army has scattered them and they are retreating to the south and west. I wonder if we will meet any of them.

May 14, Thursday — Today Mr. Ohman called the Acting Governor and his Court to the mission compound to tell them the sad news. The arrival of this large company of local government officials was not understood by the local Wallamo people. They were suspicious of foul play, so numbers of them gathered in the thickets surrounding the station armed with spears and swords. They professed concern for our safety. At ground level the outlook isn't so good, but thanks be to God, our citizenship is in heaven and He is still on the throne. What's next?

May 15, Friday — A telephone message came today from Sidamo and Alan Smith with the tragic news that my very dear friends Tom Devers and Cliff Mitchell have both been killed in the Kassi Desert. When I received a message from Mr. Duff on the 28th of April to remain quiet, I sent it on to them in Sidamo, some fifty miles east, knowing of their plans to travel to Addis Ababa. In fact, when Tommy was here three weeks ago, we made plans to travel together, to meet at the third day's camp. Now Tommy is dead, just a few miles from where we planned to meet. I just can't believe it! The rumors are that they were attacked by a large band of Arussies on the 7th and killed in the same manner as Arussies always kill their male victims.* . . . We can't understand these things. Our minds are geared to the earthly state. But one day God will make it all plain.

---

*The Arussies, like other primitive tribes elsewhere, required the male members of the tribe to kill another man before he would be permitted to marry. He was required to prove his deed by producing evidence of the emasculation of his victim, who was often killed by bleeding to death as a result of the mutilation.

May 16, Saturday — The fighting between the Amharas and the Marakos† continues, having reached Bodetti, two hours north. The first large contingent of the defeated Ethiopian army reached the Governor's palace late today. Rumor has it that they have plundered and killed all the way down from Addis Ababa. They are camped in the plain just below the Governor's old palace in clear view from our front door.

May 17, Sunday — The soldiers endeavored to break into the Government treasury today and steal the tax money. They were dissuaded by the Acting Governor from doing so. We have heard that they were given $3,000 Ethiopian instead.

May 18, Monday — We have decided that it is best to carry on our regular normal work during the day but that we should all sleep in one house at night. We are eight — Mr. and Mrs. Ohman, Dr. and Mrs. Roberts, Miss Lois Briggs, John Trewin, Alan Webb, and me. We have fortified the house by covering all openings, windows and doors, with eucalyptus poles.

May 24, Sunday — After a few days of quiet we had a bit of excitement again today. Cowna Cubba, one of the baptized believers, told us that some soldiers in the town had approached him to inquire as to where we kept our money. He told them he didn't know, and that he doubted we had very much. However, just before sundown we noticed a group of about fifty men armed with guns were gathered at the lower end of the compound, obviously waiting for darkness. Somewhere around 8 o'clock we began to hear rapid firing of shells screeching over the house. All lights were extinguished at once.

After waiting a few minutes Mr. Ohman asked Alan and me to accompany him outside to reconnoiter and see what we could find. As we crept alongside the kitchen

†There was a great deal of inter-tribal fighting during the interim between the government's collapse and the arrival of the Italians.

Barricaded window in the Ohman's house at Soddo depicts the tension of war. Davis

Ray Davis and Tommy Devers, the young missionary killed by savage tribesmen. Davis

Above, left and below: the Italian army entered Soddo with tanks, trucks and foot soldiers. Davis

near the rear of the house, we were able to observe this band of men circling the borders of the mission compound. The mission compound is enclosed by a three-foot high cornstalk fence that will burn easily and could hardly withstand the effort of a strong child to push it over. We watched them completely circle the mission compound firing their rifles at frequent intervals. After an hour or so, during which time they were obviously arguing amongst themselves as to what to do, judging by their loud voices, they moved off. Why they did not enter the compound and fulfill their mission, we have no way of knowing. However, we are very conscious of the presence of the Lord. It may be that He has put fear into their hearts or in some other way chosen to protect our lives.

May 28, Thursday — We live from one day to the next. This morning an Armenian merchant came over from the town very excited. He stated that the soldiers in Soddo were plotting to kill the foreigners and steal their goods. We learned this afternoon as Walde and Tushodi arrived from Gamo, that the folk down there were robbed of everything valuable they possessed. They themselves were not harmed. . . . While we are somewhat afraid, our trust and faith is still strong toward God. He has never failed in one of His promises, He will not now. Whatever the days ahead may hold, O God keep us faithful.

May 29, Friday — Today was the monthly day of prayer. Mr. Ohman and Dr. Roberts went into town at 9 o'clock to try to talk by phone with Alan Smith in Sidamo and Harold Street in Chencha and confer with the local officials. The rest of us gathered at the same time and had a wonderful time in prayer. . . . The men returned at 1:30 without having accomplished much. It was impossible to get through to Street or Smith. The Acting Governor promised police guards again. At 2 o'clock we met for our afternoon prayer session, which was excellent in spirit. Mr. Ohman read II Chronicles 20, the same chapter John Trewin read in the morning meeting, although this was unknown to Mr. Ohman. This seeming coincidence has assured us greatly. . . . The instructions to [Jehoshaphat] were, "Ye shall not need to fight in this battle; set yourselves, stand ye still . . . ."

May 30, Saturday — We are very much concerned about the folk in Gamo. We have been trying to get mule drivers and carriers to go down and help bring them up without success. A large military airplane flew over the town and station today but did not drop any bombs. This touch with the outside world left us with a nostalgic feeling. May God comfort and assure my loved ones, as by this time all the mail I have sent will have reached them.

June 7, Sunday — Numerous bands, some large, some small, of the retreating soldier army passed down the road which bisects the station. Some are friendly and some are decidedly unfriendly. I was standing in the front door of the house, facing the road, when several of the soldiers today shouted menacingly and leveled their rifles on the fence, pointing directly at us. God must have had a hold of their hands for nothing happened.

June 13, Saturday — We have all returned to our homes to sleep at night.

June 15, Monday — There was considerable unrest today. Several native friends came and whispered rumors of soldiers coming to rob us. It seems that the soldiers are revolting against the Governor and demanding that they be allowed to loot the foreigners and the customs house. The Wallamos are terrified. God has delivered us before, He can do so again now! Heard today that George, the Greek merchant from town, who left for Addis Ababa a week before I was scheduled to go, was killed near Silte. O God, how kind and loving and faithful Thou hast been to Thy servant. May I ever be faithful to Thee! Laid the inside brick walls of the nurses' home today.

June 19, Friday — Many more groups have passed right through our station. They have plundered and killed until they reached us and began again immediately they passed by, although they went through the station in a very orderly manner. Praise God, His legions are guarding us, His presence overshadows in a very real way these days. . . . The nurses' home is finished with the exception of plaster.

June 20, Saturday — The Forsbergs arrived from Gofa today having made the journey in six and one-half days. Mrs. Forsberg is expecting their first little one and has appendicitis, needing an operation. [The operation, the first major operation in the surgical block of the new hospital, was successfully performed by Dr. Roberts.]

June 28, Sunday — A quiet day for us but with many of the Wallamos on the hill going off to the war in Marako. Yesterday the Governor made a proclamation that every man big enough to throw a spear was to go to war on penalty of being hung in the market place if he refused. Groups of fifteen to twenty-five men left about noon.

July 4, Saturday — I hope the 4th was more pleasant at home than it was here, for it poured "buckets" all day long. Webby [Alan Webb] and I went out on our animals hoping to meet the Street party coming up from Gamo, but did not find them. Later in the afternoon they arrived very bedraggled, extremely weary and soaked through to the skin.

July 5, Sunday — We are becoming quite a young colony now. Mal Forsberg preached this evening on II Chronicles 20. This makes the third time that this chapter has been brought to our attention, each time by one to whom it was unknown that it had been spoken on before.

July 8, Wednesday — Webby is sick in bed with laryngitis. He feels pretty miserable and quacks like a duck. This morning he washed his teeth and the servant boy took the pitcher out to empty it. Thinking it would not be right to waste the contents since they were, as he supposed, epsom salts, he drank the waste water in which Webby had brushed his teeth. He denied it, but after kidding him awhile he admitted that he had swallowed a good bit of it.

July 11, Saturday — Finished the laying of the mud bricks this morning. Worked hard all day on the hospital; and quite weary tonight and kinda lonesome. It is more than ten weeks now since the last mail arrived on April 29th.

July 27, Monday — Mr. Ohman and Dr. Roberts went up to visit the Governor. He asked us why we were selling clothes and other articles. When told that our food and money were nearly gone he stated that he was very sorry that he had not known, and that he would be glad to send us some. About 5:30 several of his servants came to the station with a huge fatted ox from the Governor's own herd.

August 10, Monday — Two postmen arrived from Jimma this morning with news from Addis Ababa. This is the first break in fifteen weeks with no word from the outside world.

October 27, Tuesday — Many Amhara soldiers fleeing from Sidamo have arrived. They are living in Wallamo huts but appear to be quite orderly. Some of the old Wallamo men nearby came to Mr. Ohman. They said they feared we would all be robbed and that we should flee with them down below Humbo, a mountain visible from here four or five hours journey to the south. At a meeting of the station we all felt we should stay here until the Lord definitely told us to leave. We have repeatedly had the assurance from the Lord, II Chronicles 20 and other portions, that we were to stay here and sit still . . . .

November 23, Monday — Mr. Ohman, Dr. Roberts and I went into town to buy anything we could find to eat since the town merchants are leaving for Jimma. They were in a state of fright, not knowing what to do, but afraid to stay and afraid to go since the road is so dangerous.

November 27, Friday — Today is the monthly day of prayer. Word was received through one of the town merchants that permission had come for them to sell to us the stores of flour and sugar in the Greek merchant's store. This is an answer to prayer and we are very happy, even though we are not at all sure in what condition these supplies will be found.

When finally the bags of flour were procured they were found to be full of weevils and worms. They were, to begin with, a very poor grade of flour used by the Greek merchant as filler in the manufacture of soap. They had by this time been stored in this damp storeroom for over a year and hence tasted very mouldy and unpalatable. We carefully screened the flour, and spread it out on grass mats in the sun to dry to remove, if possible, some of the mouldy taste and smell.

There is more to the diary, of course — the details of marvelous deliverances as well as interesting experiences are a record of God's providential care and loving concern for a young missionary. They reveal the means God chose to show the Wallamo believers an example in real life of how the Christian should conduct himself in the face of difficulty, danger and death. There can be no doubt that God used these months of anxiety and privation, along with the tragic deaths of two of our number, to fortify the Wallamos for what He knew was coming all too soon.

The remaining days of the year were filled with rumors, threats of danger, much anxiety and many thrilling experiences which testify to the keeping power of our God. As the dry season came on the Italian armies were able to advance, and by the close of the year were very near Soddo. Repeated bombings of the town and surrounding area, machine gun strafing and the dropping of pamphlets with appeals to surrender demoralized the populace — even the Governor.

Our staple food supply had long since run out completely. Normally such supplies were purchased in Addis Ababa and shipped in by mule caravan twice a year, just before and after the rainy season. We were too late to receive our semi-annual supply before the country became unsettled due to the collapse of the government. Consequently we had to live off the land. The last mail which we received included a good supply of garden seeds, which proved to be a godsend. In order to make these seeds grow during the dry season when it would not normally be possible, God sent occasional rains out of season. Several times the Governor sent fatted oxen down to give us meat. This meant for several days we would have all the meat we could possibly eat, and some to share with our immediate friends. (Having no refrigeration whatsoever, it was impossible to keep it very long.) Fellow-believers among the Wallamos also helped us, out of their meager fare.

At last on January 19, 1937, the Italian armies entered and occupied Soddo town and environs. This meant for us the end of our long siege of jeopardy and anxiety of evil-doing at the hands of others. The Italians were quite friendly to us, gave us food, and some of the soldiers bought things from us when it became apparent that we would not be staying on much longer.

10 ⌒ Toro

WHHOOOMMPPHH! Crash! Clatter! Bang!!!
From the hospital building at the lower end of the mission compound I looked back at my house. Grass and sticks of wood seemed to be erupting behind it. I dropped my tools and ran. When I had left the house for work that morning there had been only one door in the small grass hut that served as a kitchen. Now there were two!

Toro had been preparing my dinner in a large pressure cooker on the stove made of three stones covered with a piece of sheet-iron. Although he had been repeatedly instructed to be very cautious about opening the belt which kept the top and bottom of the pressure cooker together before it had cooled off, unfortunately this time Toro had forgotten. With the belt partially loosened, the pressure cooker had exploded, and the top had gone clean through the roof, narrowly missing Toro's face and head. The regular door was too far away for him; he wanted to get out of there fast — so he made his own door. A badly scared Toro appeared sometime later.

99

When he had overcome his fear and apprehension, he said, "Godo (master), I do not understand."

"Toro, you do not have to understand. All you have to do is follow instructions. The operation of this cooker is not a complicated device, but you must observe the few simple rules whether you understand them or not, or you will suffer for it. You don't have to understand; just obey — that's all."

Toro had heard the Gospel as a lad and through the early years of his life had worked for different missionaries. There was no doubt that he truly loved the Lord, but he was one of those individuals with a propensity for getting himself involved in trouble, sometimes his own. When he married a lovely young Wallamo girl we thought that there was real hope for Toro to settle down.

But when he took a second wife, we all gave him up. That is, everyone except the Lord. One night, not long after his second marriage, Toro's house caught fire and burned to the ground with all his possessions. No one was hurt, but this and succeeding misfortunes humbled Toro, and he sincerely repented, putting away the second wife. Now for several years he had lived consistently. He was zealous in his witness and was very faithful in his attendance at the Bible study class held four times a week by Mr. Ohman.

Toro was working for me as a cook. To designate him as such was actually a great misnomer, but of the two of us he came the closer. One evening in February, 1937, after the meal was finished and the dishes washed and put away, Toro came in as usual for Bible reading and prayer before going to his home. When prayers were over he remained seated on the stool near the fireplace. A troubled look darkened his face. He repeatedly glanced up, then dropped his head to study his hands tightly clasped before him.

We had learned long since never to hurry such a friend to tell you what was on his heart. He will tell you when he gets ready. Finally, Toro looked up and with resolution written all over him, he said, "Master, I wish you would dismiss me from my work."

Nothing could have surprised me more than such a request. It was apparent to all of us, missionaries and believers, that the Italian government would not tolerate us indefinitely. Eventually we would be forced to leave the country. This had been the practice of the Italians in their other African colonies, and there was little evidence in their present action to show it would be any different in Ethiopia. The day they entered Soddo, the army had occupied our mission hospital. The first Sunday of their occupation a priest had held mass in the open square before the hospital.

So I argued with Toro. "Why are you asking to be dismissed now, Toro? It may be that eventually I will have to leave, and you will no longer have work, but it would be difficult for me to have you go now. I have no one else who can help me in looking after the house and the preparation of my food while I am busy working on the hospital."

"Yes, Master, all that you say it true. Sometime, perhaps, you missionaries will leave Wallamo. That is just the reason why I feel that I should now return to my home in Koisha" (the valley beyond this next mountain range to the west), explained Toro.

"What has that got to do with it, Toro?" I asked. "Can't you wait until that time comes before returning home? As you say, it may not be very long."

"Master, if I wait until you leave and then return to my people, they will say that I worked as long as I could for the white man to enjoy the money he paid me. If I try to witness to them and preach the Gospel they will not listen. But if I return to my people now, while I still have the opportunity of working for you and earning money, they will not be able to say this. I will be free to preach to them and they must listen. You know that in all the valley where I live there are no believing people. For many days now God has been speaking to me about this, and I must go."

As I looked into Toro's face I saw that he was speaking the truth.

"Toro, have you thought this through? You have not farmed. You have no granary. You have no money saved with which to feed yourself and your family until the harvest comes."

"All that you say it true, Master, but surely God will provide. Have we not often read in God's Word of His provision for his people? Have you not often yourself told me how God has provided all your need, though you are living far from home and in a strange country?"

"There is no denying that. God will provide for you. But before you leave shall we pray again?"

We bowed our heads and Toro prayed first, simply, in childlike faith asking God to provide what he needed in order to do what God had asked him to do. He thanked the Lord for hearing his prayer.

When he finished I continued to pray for him and for God's provision. It was now only the middle of the dry season. Toro, I knew, had no store of grain for him and his family to live on until the next harvest. I knew that of the small pittance I paid him for working, there was nothing left.

Then, as I prayed, there came before my mind a picture of the little cloth bag that lay in the top tray of my trunk in the adjoining room. In this small bag I knew were five round shiny silver Ethiopian dollars ($2.00 U.S.). As I continued to pray it became apparent to me that God was going to answer Toro's prayer, and that he was going to do it with my money.

Toro and his wife left a paying job with the missionaries to preach the Gospel to his own people. **Davis**

Below, Toro and his family — wife, child and mother. **SIM**

On and on I prayed, meanwhile reasoning with the Lord that this money was all that I possessed. Most likely, it was all that I would be able to obtain for some time, since it had been procured through barter (our channel of supply from the capital had not yet opened up after the siege). However, more and more strongly the Lord impressed upon my mind that this was the way He had chosen to supply Toro's need, so I finally concluded what was becoming a prolonged prayer.

Standing to my feet I walked into the adjoining room and got the little white bag. As I returned to the room and stood before Toro I emptied the five dollars from the bag into his two outstretched hands. When he saw what I had done, his big black eyes glistened. Springing to his feet, he shouted, "Master, you cannot afford to do this! I know that this is all the money you have. Your need is great as well as mine."

"Toro, God spoke to me while I was praying, asking Him to meet your need. He said that He would meet your need and that He would do it with this money. Therefore, take it. We know that God will meet my need too, somehow, some way."

A few moments later, Toro, most grateful and deeply touched, slipped out of the door and into the darkness. Early the next morning before daylight, with his wife and little child he was on the path back to his village and people.

We saw Toro only twice after that before we had to leave Soddo. It was long enough, however, for us to see how right he had been in leaving the mission station work and returning to his own people to witness to them. Within weeks God began to speak to his friends and relatives.

One of the very first converts Toro won was Cowna Gafato.* He had talked to him once only, when Gafato queried him.

When the Wallamos go to their witch doctors they can never

---

*Cowna means "King's Son." All Cownas are said to come from the Wallamo king's line.

get finished at one visit. Sometimes they have to come back again and again. So when Gafato, who was accustomed to communing with the witch doctors, heard such marvelous words from Toro, he likened it to the wisdom of the witch doctors.

Toro answered his question, "Do we eat food every day or just certain days?"

Gafato answered, "Every day we eat."

"All right, then you can come at any time, and I will give you the Word of God."

It was on a Friday that Gafato first heard the gospel message. He was so impressed with what he heard, and what it had evidently meant to Toro, that he brought ten other men with him on the following Sunday. Again and again he returned bringing others with him to hear the message of salvation, spending every possible moment he was free with Toro. It seemed as though his heart was as dry as the dust at the end of the dry season. He soon became thoroughly convinced that this message was what he had been searching for and he embraced the Lord Jesus Christ "with both hands." Twelve weeks later he was baptized.

Ato Biru, the church leader at Soddo, was a bit skeptical when he heard that Gafato had been baptized just three months after he believed.

"How is it that you can be baptized so soon?" he asked Gafato. "We usually like to see the candidates for a longer period in the church and hear their testimony before they take the step of baptism."

"But," Toro interrupted, "you do not need to wait any longer for him. He knows the Lord. He really believes."

Toro was right. It wasn't long before others, seeing the change in Gafato, believed in Jesus Christ who had changed him. Gafato's wife, along with many others, was baptized, and a small church started.

11 — 'Til We Meet Again

*. . . he hath said, I will never leave thee, nor for-
sake thee.*

— Hebrews 13:5

EARLY IN THE MORNING of April 17, 1937, Italian
army trucks came to take us and our few belongings to Addis
Ababa. There were 26 of us going — 19 missionaries and seven
children. The trucks were part of an army convoy, and the
officers insisted we leave promptly. But it was most difficult
to break away — to make the last embrace, the last handshake.
There were tears and "God be with you tell we meet again."
When would we meet again?

The trucks began to pull away from the mission station.
We looked back at the Wallamo Christians standing with the
Ohmans who were to be flown out by way of Jimma in a few
days. How few they were, how frail! And now to be left alone
again, as they had been for centuries, after so brief a decade.
But what a difference now!

When the missionaries came in 1928 there was not a single
Wallamo believer, nothing of the Bible in their language, no
knowledge of Jesus and the new life that comes through

believing in Him. Now, after just nine years, there was a small church — part of the invisible body of Christ. A group of forty-eight baptized believers were all living witnesses of the tremendous change the Gospel had made in Wallamo life.

As we turned the last corner around the mountain and saw in the distance the wave of their hands in farewell, we wondered what would happen to the little flickering flame of gospel light that had been lit in the midst of so much darkness. Would these young Christians, with no more of the Word of God in their own language than the Gospel of Mark and a few small booklets of selected Scripture portions to guide and teach them, be able to stand under the persecution that would inevitably come?

When the order had come from the American and British Embassies in July, 1935, to evacuate all missionary personnel, there were only seventeen baptized believers in Wallamo. But the missionaries chose to remain among the people, giving up any protection their governments might afford. Because we knew the time was short we did everything we could to teach the Christians and get the gospel message out. Daily Bible classes were held at Biru's home during the months of the siege and the Italian occupation. It was unsafe to leave the mission compound, but the urgency and importance of using the little time which remained to further train the young Christians warranted the danger.

Now the little group had grown to forty-eight and the church was well organized. There was no question whom we thought should become their leader. However, we wanted to trust the Lord to lead them directly in making their own choice. We demonstrated how to vote by secret ballot and to our great joy Biru was unanimously chosen.

On the day before we left Wallamo, all of us met for a last time of fellowship around the Lord's Table. The reality of the presence of the Lord made our hearts overflow with praise and gratitude. But the painful sorrow at the prospect of separation and our expectation of never meeting again this side of heaven made this occasion impossible to duplicate. Final exhortations and words of encouragement were given. We emphasized that this was now the work of the Wallamos entirely, and that if their fellow tribespeople were to hear the Gospel they must be faithful in their speaking to others. If they withheld this good news, God would hold them responsible. We assured them, God willing, we would, if possible, return again, but if not, we would meet them at Jesus' feet.

We were remembering this farewell meeting with its mingled joy and sorrow as the trucks lumbered down the road kicking up great clouds of dust. We knew that God was faithful, and He was able to preserve what He had begun among the Wallamos. But still we wondered — if we ever come back, what will we find?

12 ~ But God

*. . . they continued stedfastly in the apostles' doc-
trine and fellowship, and in breaking of bread, and
in prayers.*

— Acts 2:42

"WHEN YOU MISSIONARIES LEFT, it was difficult
to find a Christian in Wallamo country. Now it is difficult to
find a man who is not a Christian."

Hardly believing what they heard, Laurie and Lillie Davison
looked questioningly around the group of Wallamos seated in
front of their fireplace in Addis Ababa. Such a sweeping statement — how could it be true? Perhaps it was just a good
Wallamo story. Was it really possible that the gospel light had
not been snuffed out but was blazing more strongly than ever?

Questioning the Wallamo visitors only magnified the original
statement to greater proportions. Yes, great numbers of Wallamo
people had turned to the Lord. The village life — in fact the
entire tribal life of the southern country had been transformed.
There were now perhaps 100 separate churches, and probably
10,000 believers in Wallamo.

From 48 to 10,000 — an increase of 20,000%! It seemed even

more incredible when the Davisons remembered how little of the Scriptures had been translated into Wallamo, and how few Wallamos could read either their own language or Amharic. But the more they questioned the Wallamo visitors who had traveled up to Addis Ababa to see them, the more wonderful the story seemed.

The year was 1942. Ethiopia was beginning to recover from the shock of war, but as yet no missionaries had been allowed to return. Laurie Davison was in the group that had opened the work in Gofa in the early 30's. Now he and Lillie were in Addis Ababa with the British Ministry of Education, as part of the Occupied Enemy Territory Administration. Their presence there and meeting with the Wallamos seemed almost as marvelous as the reports they were hearing.

When the Emperor fled the country in 1936, his return looked utterly impossible. The League of Nations did not respond to his appeal for help. His warning to the League sounded a prophetic note:

> It is my duty to inform the governments of the deadly peril which threatens them. . . . It is a question of trust in international treaties and the value of promises to small states that their integrity shall be respected.

> In a word, it is international morality that is at stake. Apart from the Kingdom of God, there is not on this earth any nation that is higher than another. . . . God and history will remember your judgment.

But the way back was shorter and quicker than anyone had expected. When Italy entered the Second World War in 1940, North Africa became a part of the sphere of fighting. British forces from Africa and Europe, supported by Ethiopian patriots, defeated the Italians in Ethiopia, and Haile Selassie became the first deposed monarch of the war to be restored to his throne.

On May 5, 1941, exactly five years from the day that he left, the Emperor re-entered Addis Ababa. In his speech to his liberated people, he encouraged them to begin the work of reconstruction and development. In a noble gesture he refused revenge and urged restraint toward the defeated enemy.

> Do not reward evil for evil. Do not commit any acts of cruelty like those which the enemy committed against us.

To the credit of the Ethiopian people, and contrary to what one might expect in view of the atrocities committed against them, there was no seeking of revenge on the Italian people, civilian or military.

In his effort to restore peaceful conditions to the country, the Emperor was helped by the British military authorities who had made possible his return. The British were in Ethiopia to finish the war in North Africa, so there was quite a period of time during which a quasi-military occupation hastened stability and prosperity.

The Davisons had spent the years of the Italian occupation in Khartoum, capital city of the neighboring Anglo-Egyptian Sudan. When he learned that he could return to Ethiopia by joining the British Army, Laurie Davison immediately applied and was accepted. For a while he traveled around the country with the Army. When conditions began to return to normal he was able to transfer from the military forces to the Ministry of Education and both he and his wife took positions in schools in Addis Ababa.

Then Laurie was given command of an Ethiopian soldier repatriation camp in the capital. There he found many Wallamo soldiers waiting to return to their homes. Since he was able to speak their language, it was easy to make friends with them. Before long, Christians in Wallamo heard that former missionaries were living in the capital. Many of the church elders walked the long distance from Wallamo country to see the Davisons.

So it was around their own fireside that the Davisons began to hear from the Wallamo Christians what had happened in the five years since the missionaries had left. They also learned of some of the problems that had arisen in the church because of their lack of Scripture knowledge.

One of the Davison children came bounding into the living room one evening, followed by the family dog. The small terrier ran up to the visitors in friendly dog fashion, but the Wallamos shrank back as though they were afraid.

"You don't need to be afraid of this little thing," Laurie Davison said laughingly. "He won't hurt you. The children play with him all the time, and he's quite friendly."

It was not a question of being afraid of the dog, one of the Christians replied. But they understood that Christians should not have dogs in their homes.

"Where did you learn that? Why do you say Christians should not have dogs?"

"Do we not read in the New Testament," said one of the elders, "that Paul told the believers, 'Beware of dogs'?"

While the Davisons explained the meaning of that phrase, they began to realize that even the simplest statements in the New Testament would need to be talked over with the Wallamo Christians, who took everything at face value.

When Dr. Bingham heard of the amazing growth of the Wallamo church, he decided to go to Ethiopia immediately to see for himself. The opening of southern Ethiopia to the Gospel had been a dream of his — and here was its fulfillment. He was also anxious to negotiate with the Ethiopian government for the reopening of missionary work in the country. Just before he was to leave Canada, however, he was taken ill and died on December 8, 1942.

It was July 1, 1943, before his successor, Guy Playfair, was able to carry out the visit to the interior of Ethiopia. Heading south out of Addis Ababa with two former missionaries (who had never worked in Wallamo but knew the area fairly well), they traveled by truck over rough roads for three days. Finally on the evening of the third day they stopped at the home of a Christian in a village five miles from Soddo. Immediately the word went from farmhouse to farmhouse, spreading farther and farther — "The missionaries have returned!" There was little sleep for anyone that night.

How can one describe the feeling of the Christians? Here was a whole community, an entire tribe, that had heard the Gospel. Thousands had believed the message in spite of persecution. All thought of the missionaries as those "who had brought us God's matter" — but none of them, even those who had known the missionaries, ever expected to see missionaries again. "Our only hope, we thought, was to meet you in God's country," they said.

But now, unexpectedly, here the missionaries were.

By daylight the next morning, Sunday, July 4, the Christians were already gathering, coming by scores and hundreds from every direction to see the missionaries with their own eyes.

"Are they really ours?"

"Have they come from heaven?"

"Are we dreaming?"

"Welcome! Welcome!"

"Oh, to have known the language of this happy people," was Mr. Playfair's reaction.

After the morning worship service, a call was sent out for the leaders of the more than 100 churches to meet with the missionaries for a three-day conference, beginning Tuesday. In the meantime the visitors were kept busy, meeting with more of the Christians. In one large church approximately four hundred gathered to worship with them.

By Tuesday evening seven hundred church leaders had come from every part of Wallamo to take part in this church council, which reminded Mr. Playfair and his party of the early church meeting in Acts 15.

The three days were spent in considering some of the problems that had arisen because of the mushrooming growth of the church and the lack of Bible teaching, and in learning something of what the Christians experienced under the Italians.

For instance, there was the Friday prayer meeting. This had begun during a time of persecution when fifty of the church leaders had been imprisoned. The Christians began to meet together every Friday to pray for the prisoners, and to fast. The practice became a custom which continued even after the leaders were released. And before long, the natural Wallamo tendency toward ritual and the ceremonial keeping of days turned the custom into a legalistic snare. But when the clear teaching of the Scriptures about legalism and the observance of special days was pointed out, the response of the leaders was wholehearted and immediate. There was never any question about following the New Testament literally and absolutely, when its teachings were understood.

Questions about drinking beer, eating raw meat, the use of tobacco had brought division between the Wallamo church and the church among the neighboring Hadiyas to the north. A few Hadiya Christians had accompanied the missionary party into Wallamo from Kambatta. They presented their point of view. The Wallamo church had decided against these practices without hesitation, but there was less clear definition about them among the Hadiyas. As a result of this council meeting, fellowship between the two churches was restored, although the Hadiya church did not take the absolute stand against beer and tobacco of the Wallamo church. As for eating raw meat, the Christians were advised against it purely on hygienic grounds — but it should not hinder anyone from being baptized. Polygamy had never presented a problem — the church had unanimously decided against baptizing polygamists.

A problem which threatened to divide the Wallamo church itself was the matter of church leadership and discipline. There was a tendency for groups to follow their own local leaders, much like the first-century church in Corinth, and there was disagreement as to who should baptize and administer the Lord's supper. Questioning revealed that the church did not consider the local church elders to have equal authority with the three chosen before the missionaries left. Men like Toro, Gafato and Wandaro who had started churches or were elders in their local churches did not share in the direction of the whole church.

When it was pointed out that if a church of 50 members had needed three elders in the beginning, 100 churches would need at least 300 elders — or three for each local church — the Wallamos saw the point. Each church then selected its own elders, men who had proved faithful according to Biblical standards, all to have equal authority.

The churches were roughly divided into three districts, and in order to lead more effectively, the elders appointed men from each district to a joint council which would meet periodically for fellowship and advice.

As they listened to the stories of the occupation, Mr. Playfair and his companions were overwhelmed by the sufferings the Wallamos had endured for Christ's sake. At one point the 50 leaders had been arrested and put in prison when the Italians realized that their efforts to stamp out the church were only increasing its strength and size. Each of the leaders received 100 lashes, and one was given 400. None of them were able to lie on their backs for months, and three died. When the priest offered them instant freedom if they would only kiss the crucifix, all of them refused the offer. They realized that they were in prison for religious rather than political reasons, and they preferred to die rather than to deny their faith.

It was several years, however, before the full story of the church in the occupation could be pieced together from fragments collected here and there in conversation.

PART V
BAPTIZED BY FIRE

13 ～ The Fire Spreads

. . . having received the word in much affliction,
with joy of the Holy Ghost . . . from you sounded
out the word of the Lord . . .

— I Thessalonians 1:6, 8

"As a bomb bursts and spreads fire, so the Word of God burst and began to spread throughout Wallamo."

That was the way the Christians described the growth of the church after the missionaries left.

But the first few months did not produce any startling changes. Before we left them we had increasingly emphasized their responsibility to reach their own people with the Gospel, and they were already speaking more boldly about Jesus Christ. They were also meeting together in their own rather widely scattered communities for prayer and church services — due primarily to the refusal of the Italians to allow any Wallamo meetings on the mission station.

"We are leaving you, but God will not leave you," had been our parting words to them. Yet we would not have been completely surprised if they had become discouraged and given up at the first sign of difficulty. The first three months on their

119

own were a time of testing and self-examination with a great
deal of prayer.

Then the fire came. Or, as Ato Ginja described it, "As
thirsty cattle turn toward the tasty water, so the people began
to turn to God. They left their Satan worship and pagan
practices."

The tiny churches began sending out preachers, two by two,
baptizing those who had believed for some time. Soon even
the unbelievers were eager to hear God's Word. As many
hundreds turned to God, branch churches were established.
By the second year it was necessary to build church buildings
and choose local elders.

Looking back on these days, one can see the strategy of
the Holy Spirit for the church. He raised up strong, individualistic, courageous personalities, through whom He eventually
caused the Gospel to move like wildfire throughout the land
of the Wallamos. Dana Maja was one of these — Biru another.

Biru was readily recognized by the Christians as their leader.
He had somewhat more understanding of the Scriptures, as
well as the ability to read the Amharic Bible, so he was the
natural one to whom the people turned. Then, too, he was a
bit older than the more aggressive younger men and this also
pointed to him as the logical leader.

The Christians began coming in large numbers to Biru's
home for teaching and help in learning to read. They never
came empty-handed, but would bring donkey-loads of wood,
grain, butter, and every once in a while a sheep. After a
while they came once a week to keep his fences in repair and
work in his fields; in fact they were prepared to do anything
that might be asked of them. With churches springing up in
different parts of the province, Biru was kept busy making
constant rounds to visit them, so the believers bought him a
horse.

Within two years after the missionaries left, Dana Maja was made an elder in his local church several miles south of Soddo. Then came severe persecution. The local believers had erected a large church building on land which belonged to one of the elders in Dana Maja's church. This elder became afraid at threats made against him, and requested the Christians to remove their church from his ground. Like many of the Wallamo believers, he was not well grounded in the Word of God; most of them were mere babes spiritually. With rumors rampant, this man felt he could not face the pressures and physical danger. Since fear is contagious, some of the other believers became afraid. They wanted to follow the Lord, yet dared not have a church on their own land for fear of reprisals. Seeing that all the others were afraid, Dana Maja said, "Since there is no place for the believers to meet, my house will be God's House. I have given it to Him. I and my family will move out of our large house and I will build a smaller one."

When the number of Christians became so great that they could no longer be contained in the chief's house, they met for a time in the open air in front of the house. Usually in each meeting Dana Maja would stand up and say, "Now we are all going to pray. Let everyone bow his head for prayer."

Invariably someone in the group would speak up to those around him: "Don't bow your heads. They are planning to take our mules. If you bow your heads and close your eyes, they will do it while you are not looking."

Dana Maja would reply, "Don't be afraid, my brethren. I know the Lord now. I am not the man I used to be."

Later the believers were able to erect a large church building with a grass roof, typically Wallamo style. The non-Christians were so incensed over the great numbers of their own people following this strange way, that one night they set fire to the church and burned it to the ground. Undaunted, the believers

gathered enough money, at great sacrifice, to purchase corrugated roofing iron. They built a new church building that
would not burn.

The persecutions began when the Italian authorities took
notice of the increase of Christians and the building of many
churches. At first, encouraged no doubt by the Italian priests,
they restricted the church and Christian activity. Instead of
deterring the movement, however, this only gave it impetus.
The more severe the persecutions became, the more rapidly the
young church grew.

Then the local Wallamo chiefs began to report the continued growth of the Christians to the authorities. As a result
the Italians sent police to the churches to investigate and to
arrest the leaders. When they found that the Christians prayed
for His Majesty, the exiled Emperor, they were exceedingly
angry and tore down the churches. They also tried to destroy
Bibles and Scripture portions. Some of the believers who
had Amharic Bibles or smaller Scripture portions put them in
clay pots and buried them in the ground. Others wrapped
them in wild banana leaves and hid them in the grass roofs
of their homes. The owners of the land on which churches
were built were arrested and put in prison. The persecution
became so severe that Christians began holding communion
and baptismal services at night.

At this time the Italians were looking principally for Biru
as the leading pastor, but they could not find him. For six
months the police searched for him, but he managed to hide
from them by living in forests, traveling to other districts where
he was not well known, or being hidden by believers in and
around their houses. So they arrested his wife and put her in
prison, thinking to get him through her. She was not a strong
Christian at the time, but this imprisonment strengthened
her in the faith.

When Ato Biru heard of his wife's arrest, as the Italians had hoped he came into Soddo town and gave himself up. He was immediately seized and taken into court — an Italian military tribunal. Word was passed around town that after dark that night the Italians were going to kill him. They had threatened before that they would cut him to pieces when they caught him.

Just then word came from the southwestern area of Wallamo, toward Kindo, that Amhara bandits had killed four Italians. This caused a great stir around the town, taking people's minds off Biru, and many of the Italian soldiers were dispatched to take care of that situation. By this Ato Biru's life was spared and the believers' faith strengthened.

14 ∼ Singing in Suffering

> But God hath chosen the foolish things of the
> world to confound the wise; and God hath chosen
> the weak things of the world to confound the
> things which are mighty.
>
> — I Corinthians 1:27

"DENY YOUR FAITH or suffer!" exclaimed Fiturari
Dogesa.

"Very well," replied Wandaro, "I will gladly suffer for my
Saviour."

Dogesa was an Amhara official (a Fiturari was a kind of
Lieutenant-governor) who strongly opposed the Gospel and
who lived near Wandaro's home on Mt. Humbo, 15 miles
south of Soddo. He made Wandaro the object of continual
ridicule and sought in different ways to discourage and defeat
the spread of the Gospel in his area. No matter how he tried,
though, he failed, and the frustration of his plans angered
him exceedingly.

Down through the years Wandaro had continued to grow
in his knowledge of God. He was always zealous in preaching
and witnessing, and his latent capacity for leadership became
apparent as the persecution began.

124

Wandaro's decision to suffer rather than deny Christ angered Dogesa. He ordered his servants to give Wandaro forty stripes with the cruel hippo-hide whip — a wide strip of inch-thick hippo hide cut into strands with sharp metal pieces at the end of each strand. Later, when Wandaro had recovered from the ordeal, Dogesa said, "Go home and tell the people of your congregation to bring their grass knives to the church. You will tear down the church. All of the fine fiber, the rope, and any tying material is to be cut with knives and the church is to be cut down to the ground. Get on with the job, for I am coming to your place. Be prepared. Have all of your congregation there."

Wandaro complied with the order of the chief. The neighbors and members of his congregation came to the church as they had been ordered. With obvious pleasure, Dogesa ordered them to tear down the church which they had just recently built at great expense of labor and time.

"Now, can you sing?" Dogesa asked maliciously.

"Yes, we can sing," Wandaro replied.

"All right, sing the song that the missionary taught you," was the jesting response. "Cause these men to sing the songs you have taught them in the church." So the group began to sing:

> Jesus Christ is coming again
> He is coming to take all of His children to be with Himself.
> He is coming to take us
> And there will be no more trouble there.
> There will be no more pain there.
> He is coming to take His own to be with Himself
> There will be no more trouble,
> There will be no more pain,
> There will be no more tears,
> Jesus Christ is coming to take us to be with Himself.

The singing angered Dogesa — to think these people could and would sing while they were destroying their precious building. So he ordered all the workers present, men and women, to pick up the wood of the demolished church building and carry it to his place. There they were locked up for the night. During the evening the other Christians in the area — some of them the children, wives and mothers of the imprisoned Christians — prepared food for the whole group. After dusk they brought it to them.

Throughout the night the Christians sang and encouraged one another, knowing that nothing anyone could do to them would diminish their joy in the Lord.

Next morning they were ordered out to take up their loads again. As they traveled into Soddo carrying the bundles of wood and grass on their backs and heads, they sang more songs.

> Jesus is not one who will slumber or sleep.
> *Watch and wait.*
> He is going to come when we least expect Him.
> *Watch and wait.*
> Watch for Him more than you watch for your brothers returning from a long journey.
> *Watch and wait.*
> Watch for Him more diligently than for food when you are hungry.
> *Watch and wait.*

Those they passed on the road knew that the materials they carried came from the church which they had torn down at Dogesa's orders. Yet the believers were singing and rejoicing as though it were a privilege to suffer for Jesus Christ!

In town, they laid down their loads, free to go back to their homes. The materials were made into a house for one of the important men of the town.

Wandaro was not freed, though. Dogesa took him to the market place on the edge of town with a rope tied to his wrist. In the market place he made him hold his hand up high.

"See, everyone. Look! See, Wandaro is bound. He is tied

up. Don't go to his church again to worship. He isn't there. He is tied up. Don't try to go to his place. Don't go near to that place. There is no more church there. It is broken down. The materials of that church are now doing other work. Wandaro is tied up. Don't go to worship there anymore."

But Wandaro answered loudly, "Everyone listen! Listen to me! Believe on the Lord Jesus Christ for salvation. This rope you see is not the final rope. This rope man has put on my wrist. This is not from God."

"Come and beat Wandaro," Dogesa invited the bystanders. Fearing that they might end up in Wandaro's place if they refused, many struck him with their staves and sticks. Some who could not get near enough to beat him on his body struck him on the legs as hard as they could.

Then with hands tied behind his back, Wandaro was driven ahead of Dogesa back into the town. There, before anyone else could interfere, Dogesa grabbed Wandaro by the beard. He shook Wandaro's head with violent rage, pulling some of his beard out by the roots and leaving his face torn and bleeding.

"Now, will you give up the white man's God? Now will you give up your faith?"

"No!" gasped Wandaro, "No, never! No! Why should I give up my faith?"

Again he was beaten. Watching helplessly, Wandaro's friends hid their faces and his companions cried.

Between the lashings Wandaro managed to say to his friends, "Christ was buried right in the ground, ground like we stand upon. Why do you weep? I am yet with you. Why weep? Why are you afraid? I am not afraid. Why should you weep? I am here."

"Who has taught you to be so strong?" Dogesa was still angry but puzzled.

"The missionaries taught me!" Wandaro replied clearly and strongly.

"The missionaries have gone," cried Dogesa. "Why trouble now? They aren't here to help you and strengthen you."

"That's very true, but the God who sent them is still here. It is not the missionaries I am serving. It is God whom I am serving. God is the One who has saved me. It is God who planned my salvation. It is He who is with me right here. It is He who now strengthens me. It is not the white man. It is not the missionary."

Furiously Dogesa ordered Wandaro taken back to the market to be beaten again. This time five men were ordered to beat him in turn while he lay flat on the ground. They started about three in the afternoon. As one man tired another took the whip. When darkness came they were still whipping at intervals.

Wandaro's family and friends had been watching, but as the night wore on it grew harder to see Wandaro's sufferings grow more intense, and there was nothing they could do to help. Reluctantly they turned away to spend the night elsewhere.

At last the men stopped their whipping and carried Wandaro's almost lifeless body to the prison. But in the prison he was unable to lie down — his body was too wracked with pain. So he passed the night on his knees, bracing himself with his elbows — two parts of his body which had not been flayed open. In the morning, members of his family and friends came to the prison hoping to find him there, but were not allowed in. However, they found a Christian who had been in prison the night before, and asked if Wandaro had been brought into the prison during the night.

"Yes," was the reply.

Anxiously, fearfully they asked, "How is he?"

"Very, very bad. We fear for his life, but he is still alive. However, there is little hope."

Wandaro's wife and friends brought milk and soft food which they took to the Christian brother and begged him to take it into the prison. But when the food was offered to Wandaro he could not eat it.

A long day and night followed. Wandaro still lived. When he was able to send a message to his family and friends, he said, "I think I will live. I think I will live through it. Do not fear. Do not be concerned. I am all right. The Lord is with me."

Every day for the next week, they came to the prison hoping to see him — but still were not permitted to do so. However, Wandaro sent another message: "Don't tire yourselves too much. I'll be all right. I feel much better." They did not try to visit him again.

One day about two weeks later, they learned that he was out on the road with other prisoners pushing a big barrel which they filled with water at the stream. He was required to help push the barrel up the hill — just fifteen days after the cruel beating. Those who saw him rolling the water barrel reported to his family that he was continually witnessing to the Italian guards alongside him. This alarmed some of his relatives. After all he had suffered, why should something more fearful happen now? They tried to persuade Wandaro to be less zealous in his witness. He replied, "Why do you grieve? God has not died yet. He is still with me. It is up to us to witness for the Lord as long as He allows us to be here. Why be fearful?"

For a full year he was held in prison where he continued to witness daily. It was not difficult to find him for he was always out working. Wherever anyone was heard talking, especially about Jesus Christ, it was Wandaro.

Like Joseph, Wandaro was a model prisoner. The police

officials said of him, "If he wants to go outside the prison to get some food or to do an errand, never mind, just let him go. He will come back. He will not run away. He is honest." When the guards wanted to get off duty for any reason, they let Wandaro guard the prison.

Finally he was released from prison and returned home. Dogesa was still living nearby. Not long after, he asked Wandaro to bring as many Christians as he could to help harvest his ripened grain. "I thought I could kill you," he said to Wandaro. "I tried to, but God gave you life. Now in the name of God, come and help me."

More than a hundred Christians went singing down the path that day following Wandaro — to gather in the grain for the one who had persecuted him so severely!

Later Dogesa said to Wandaro, "Return in another fifteen days with Toro, Barum and Gafato. I will call an Orthodox Coptic priest and if circumcision and drink are forbidden in the Bible, well and good. We will hear from you and we will hear from the priest. But if not, if it is not true that such is forbidden in the Bible, then three of your men will die." He spoke these strong words not knowing where he himself would be in fifteen days. A few days later while he was sitting on a chair in his home, Dogesa fell over backward and died. The great argument and discussion on circumcision and drink never came to pass.

Some time after Dogesa's death, a number of the believers from Wandaro's area went south to preach in nearby Gamo district. The chief of Gamo sent a message back to Wandaro's area and said, "Wandaro has spoiled Wallamo. Now he sends men to Gamo to spoil our place. Do away with him. Don't let him live. Do away with him. He has done much harm already."

One Sunday the believers were gathered in Wandaro's

church when thirty men armed with guns suddenly appeared. Word of their coming had reached Wandaro moments before their arrival, and he was able to slip out of the church unobserved to go into hiding as the Christians had urged. The armed men took the entire congregation and locked them up. Rather than dampening their spirits, the imprisonment and threats filled them with joy, and they sang all night long. Next morning they were sent back home.

Five days later an official appeared in the market with a proclamation. It began with a Wallamo proverb: " 'Although the queen of the locusts doesn't have wings, if left alone it will put forth wings and fly.' " To which was added: "Catch that queen of the locusts before its wings come out. Anyone who finds him will have $15 reward. Anyone who kills him will have $30."

Late that night Wandaro, his wife, and members of his congregation were traveling along a back road. They were aiming for a distant place where Wandaro might hide safely. They had just crossed another path, when two men on animals came down it, talking quite loudly. In the darkness they did not see or hear Wandaro and his party standing quite still.

"This decree that was made in our market today? Now who would the queen of the locusts be except Wandaro?"

"Surely it is Wandaro," agreed the second man. "Who else could be the queen of the locusts? That means they are searching for him here. They said anyone who sees him will have $15 and the one who kills him will have $30."

As the voices grew faint in the distance, Wandaro and his party began to move on again with thankful hearts — both for the narrow escape and for the information. They now knew of the decree that had been made in the market that day. Wandaro's decision to go into hiding was confirmed.

Many months passed before it was safe for Wandaro to

Toro and Wandaro — two leaders who could sing praises to God in spite of terrible suffering. Füssle

Wandaro and his second wife — his first wife died after the war. Füssle

Wandaro's face shows his joy in the Lord. Füssle

return to his home and church. Even in hiding, his deep and abiding faith was like a rock upholding those who had found Christ through his testimony. Hundreds of his neighbors and countrymen looked to him as their leader and guide. Possessing few of the more easily recognizable characteristics of leadership, the beauty of Wandaro's life is the unanswerable proof that God "hath chosen the weak things of the world to confound the things which are mighty; and base things of the world, and things which are despised, hath God chosen, yea, and things which are not, to bring to nought things that are:" In Wandaro God had a man, all of him, nothing held back, totally available, obedient.

During the first two years after the missionaries left, 180 people were baptized in Koisha, west of Soddo, the results mainly of Toro's and Gafato's constant witness. Then the persecution began there.

The leaders of the church, including Toro and Gafato, were seized, given 100 stripes and sentenced to prison for ten months. The prison had no floor, only the bare ground. The walls were upright eucalyptus poles, standing close together like bars, but with nothing to keep the wind from blowing between them. There were no windows, no sanitation, no food, and the prisoners were crowded into small spaces. As uncomfortable as it may have been during the day, the bitter cold of the night wind was frequently too much for the weakened prisoners, and daylight would reveal that some had died during the night.

Since no provision was made by the prison authorities for food, the Christians took the responsibility of preparing food for their leaders. Their loving concern made a great impression on the non-Christians who tried to stay at a distance from these "trouble-makers," but who could not help noticing their quality of life. The love of the Christians for one another was quite different from the usual Wallamo relationships, even of friends. As a result, many people in the community, and in the prison, believed in Jesus Christ and His power to change lives.

Because of the severe and painful experiences they went through, Gafato and Toro became very close. When they were finally released from prison, Gafato was in hiding for six months and Toro for eight months. During this time the number of baptized believers in Koisha increased to more than 400. The lives of the Wallamo Christians, lived openly before everyone both in prison and out of it, contributed as much to the growth of the church as the preaching of the Gospel. Persecution, pain, imprisonment — God used them all for His glory.

Eventually the church in Toro's home district grew to more than a thousand believers. The animosity and jealousy of the local rulers, coupled with the oppression of the Italian authorities, resulted in Toro's imprisonment once again. Once he was given forty lashes with the hippo-hide whip. As if that were not enough, an Italian officer with heavy hob-nailed boots jumped up and down on his chest until he was nearly crushed. Toro believed that his end was near.

As he lay in prison, utterly unable to move or help himself, hardly able to breathe, he received what he describes as a visitation from the Lord. It was not at night, he says, and so not a dream, but more like a vision or wonderful sight the Lord gave him. He saw the Lord Jesus Himself in an atmosphere of extreme brightness which frightened him. But Jesus spoke to him:

"Toro, do not be afraid. You are My child and My faithful servant. Let not your heart be troubled, you believe in God, believe also in Me. In My father's house are many mansions, if it were not so, I would have told you. I go to prepare a place for you, and where I am there you also one day will be."

Toro tells how he lay there very still for what must have been a long time. But never thereafter was he afraid. And slowly he recovered.

After some weeks he was released from prison. The Christians had been forbidden to preach or to rebuild their church. But, like their biblical predecessors, they felt they must obey God and do both.

When it was learned that the Christians had dared to restore their church building, the wrath of the authorities descended upon Toro and other church leaders in greatly increased intensity. They were taken to the market place, stripped naked, thrown face down in the mud, and beaten with more than one hundred stripes. In jail, they were taunted by the Italian jailers:

"Now, where is the God that can deliver you out of our hands? You will never get out of this prison alive."

Although very weak and hardly able to make his voice heard, Toro told them, "My God answers prayer — He is able to deliver me — if He chooses — and if not, He has promised to take me to heaven to be with Him there."

Some time later, a group of the believers in prison were praying together when a terrible rain and thunderstorm came up. Toro says he doesn't remember the lightning ever being more fierce or the thunder claps louder. While they were praying and singing, the wind blew with such terrific force that the entire iron roof of the prison was torn completely off. The torrents of rain pouring down onto the exposed mud walls made them crumble and melt. The prisoners were free!

Many of the non-Christian prisoners fled. The terrified jailers, convinced that the storm was the direct intervention of God on behalf of the Christian prisoners, came to Toro pleading that he pray to God to withhold His anger and fury — and they would be released. The jailers kept their word.

After one of his severe beatings Toro composed the song, "If we suffer, we will reign with Him," which became a favorite of the Christians in prison.

> If we have little trouble here, we will have little reward there.
> *We will reign.*
> Why should we not suffer a little here and now?
> *We will reign.*
> We will reign with Him through all eternity.
> *We will reign.*

PART VI
FEEDING THE FIRE

15 ～ Untangling Some Knots

*For a great door and effectual is opened unto me,
and there are many adversaries.*

— I Corinthians 16:9

T HE GOVERNOR of Wallamo was perplexed.

A strange thing had happened in Soddo town that morning of February 1945. The messengers who brought the startling news had just left his office. He sat now, quietly and thoughtfully considering its significance.

Spread out before him on the long table which served as his desk were important looking government papers, letters bearing colorful stamps and wax seals. Important or not, the Governor's attention was now focused entirely upon the news he had just received. The messengers had reported the hatching of a chick with four legs. This was indeed an extraordinary event and something that could not simply be ignored.

Shrugging his shoulders and with an air of resignation which might be interpreted as an acceptance of the inevitable, he clapped his hands sharply to call his office clerk and slumped back into his chair.

"Allow the foreigners to enter," he sighed.

But when Laurie and Lillie Davison and their two daughters entered the room, followed by Selma Bergsten and Alfred Roke, the Governor was sitting sternly erect, with an air of importance if not impatience. As they came through the doorway he stood to his feet, unsmiling, and gently bowing in the manner of Ethiopian courtesy and greeting, motioned them to chairs which had been brought for their use.

There was a period of brief though awkward silence before the Governor began to speak. He asked what business had brought them to him so early on such a miserably wet and cold morning. Mr. Davison laid the travel papers before him for his consideration explaining that they had just the day before arrived in Soddo and were planning now to remain and take up residence in the area. Here were their travel permits, their papers of identification. The Governor carefully examined the papers and appeared to be studiously scrutinizing them to ascertain their validity. It was evident that missionaries and missionary work were something with which he was not too familiar. The puzzled expression on his face led the missionaries to believe that either there was something quite out of order regarding their papers or something else was troubling the Governor's mind.

Suddenly, in the midst of the conversation relating to their arrival and projected stay, the Governor referred to the chicken with four legs. If the missionaries were mystified by this news, much more was the Governor. He kept studying them carefully, evidently trying to straighten things out in his own mind. What possible significance or relation might the freak chicken born in the town that morning have with the coming of these foreigners? Was there any connection at all, and if so what was it? Such an extraordinary event must have some sinister meaning. The unseen world was possibly seeking to convey a message of great importance and had chosen this strange means of communicating the message by the arrival of a chicken with four legs. This would surely call for the most careful consideration.

The missionaries could only interpret the governor's strange behavior as hostility on his part toward their coming. They sat there prayerfully, anxious and concerned that their residence permits be granted. They were intrigued, too, at this interesting sidelight on the character of an important, possibly sophisticated man of authority. By his carefully phrased questions it was evident that he was paying much more attention to the voice of the unseen or spirit world, as it appeared to him, than he was to the official documents spread out before him.

Eventually, after the missionaries made several more visits for further consultation, the Governor consented to allow them to remain in the area — at least temporarily. Although the authorities in Addis Ababa had given them permission to return to Wallamo and to occupy the former mission station buildings, the local officials had different ideas. They would not allow them to take over the former mission property. So the missionaries rented a house in Soddo, a mile or more from the mission station. The ultimate fate of the freak chicken, or the supposed connection of the missionaries with it, was never known.

A few weeks later Emperor Haile Selassie visited Soddo. There were days of reconstruction and reorganization in Ethiopia, and a great deal of work needed to be done. The Emperor and other high government officials were busy traveling from one part of the country to another, trying to restore order and to set up the administrative processes. During the several days that the king was in Soddo, he held long conferences with the Governor and other local Wallamo leaders.

Throughout the period of Italian occupation the mission

station site had been used as an Italian hospital. Although they had made some minor alterations, the Italians had left things essentially as they had found them. Now through disuse and squatter-occupation, everything looked quite dilapidated and in bad repair. The Emperor and his retinue walked back and forth over the entire area of the former mission property. Yet for some undisclosed reason he declined to give the missionaries permission to return and occupy the station.

"Unknown to us," Laurie Davison later reported, "the Governor was working in close cooperation with those who wanted to counteract the influence and spread of the Gospel among the Wallamo people. This may have been largely responsible for his apprehension and unfriendliness at the time of our arrival and the suspected evil portent of the strange phenomenon of the four-legged chicken."

Shortly before the Emperor's visit, two Wallamo women, both wives of the same man, had heard the Gospel and decided to follow this new Way. Their decision greatly displeased their husband. He was a member of the Orthodox Church, so he asked the priest's help in making his wives change their minds. But the women refused to take part in the worship of the Orthodox Church. Their refusal stirred considerable opposition — enough to commit them to prison where they were actually confined with chains. All the Christians in Wallamo had been praying for their release.

At the time of the Emperor's visit, the missionaries first learned of the confinement of these believing women. A member of the Emperor's party was an old friend of the missionaries, and was staying with them. Mr. Davison had opportunity to mention to him the fact that the Wallamo women believers were kept in chains. The official demanded more details which were soon related to the Emperor. When His Majesty learned that the two women were in chains, he threw up his hands in horror. Men in prison were sometimes put in chains, but never women!

The Emperor commanded the women to be brought before him. Carefully questioning and assuring them kindly, he ordered their immediate release. He took the opportunity to make a public statement to the hundreds of people present who had followed the women to the Emperor's court. The king proclaimed that there was now to be religious liberty throughout his land. This unforeseen intervention of the Emperor surprised and greatly displeased the Governor and antagonized the priests of the Orthodox Church even more.

"Nevertheless," explained Laurie Davison, "we felt that making the plight of the imprisoned women known was something that needed to be done. We realized it might very well jeopardize our position, but we were led to go ahead with it. The Lord has subsequently vindicated this venture of faith and trust in Him. This also served to strengthen the faith of the Wallamo believers and encouraged them to continue in prayer for the many others imprisoned for the sake of their faith in Christ."

Down through the years believers have been apprehended and imprisoned, generally on trumped-up charges, evidently because of their preaching of the Gospel. Whenever appeal has been made to the Emperor he has always been most sympathetic and helpful in obtaining their release. As far as he is concerned, and officially as far as the constitution of the country is concerned, there is religious liberty. However in reality, in many places — and the more so as the area concerned is remote from the central government — there is still great difficulty and much opposition at times.

"We thought it would not be until we were in heaven," said the Wallamo believers to Walter and Marcella Ohman

His Imperial Majesty, Hailie Selassie I.
Niger-Challenge

Below, looking up along the mission station to Mount Damota. SIM—A. Kliewer

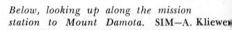

These two women, wives of the same man, were chained and imprisoned for believing in Jesus Christ. The Emperor had them released. Füssle

Soddo mission station in 1936, looking downhill. Missionaries' houses cluster to the left, the nurses' residence is going up in the center, the hospital is right. Davis

An aerial view of the Soddo mission station, about 1960. The hospital is the cluster of buildings at top left center. SIM

Wallamo church elders study the Bible by the light of a home-made lantern. Füssle

and Selma Bergsten, when they returned to Wallamo. "When you left us we said we would never see you again down here, not until we met in God's country."

By the time the Ohmans arrived in Soddo in July, 1945, there were 15,000 baptized believers in Wallamo. Among them were many who had known the missionaries in the early days, even though at that time they were not believers. Their joy now in coming to tell them that they, too, had come to know Christ as Saviour was irresistible.

During the Italian occuption years, the Ohmans had served in the Sudan among the Mabans. Now with the door to Ethiopia open once again, they returned to the land of their first love.

Since the old mission compound was still not available when they first returned to Soddo, they joined the Davisons in Soddo, renting temporary quarters in the town. The missionaries were virtually house-prisoners — forbidden to travel about the countryside to visit the churches. But no restrictions were placed upon the people, and so the Christians came by the hundreds to visit their beloved spiritual parents. By actual count, in one month more than 1500 visitors came to welcome the missionaries back. Some had walked many miles.

Confinement to the town was actually a blessing in disguise, since it provided the opportunity to conduct Bible classes day and night. To make the most of the time and to accomplish something of real and lasting value, the Bible teaching was organized to help as many as possible.

The rented house in which the Ohmans were living had three rooms. They would invite a group of fifteen men to come in from a different district each night, Monday through Friday, although more often thirty came. There would be several hours of Bible study, and then the men would spend the night sleeping on the floor of the kitchen and dining room.

In the morning, they would have another hour or so of Bible study before returning to their homes.

Often their studies together in the Word of God dealt with problems of church government and discipline that had risen during the absence of the missionaries. Yet in spite of many minor irregularities, due to the lack of the Word of God in their own language, the purity of doctrine and of living among the believers was remarkable, showing that the Holy Spirit was able to teach these simple folk directly.

"Many were the questions that we were called upon to answer," Walter Ohman recalls. "One day a man came in a great quandary to ask why at certain times the church services were held in secret. It appeared that once a month at the church services all unbelievers were asked to leave the building. Since he was not a believer, he was asked to leave the church, although his wife was permitted to remain in the meeting, because she was a believer. 'What goes on when some of us are asked to leave the meeting?' was his question.

"Up to this time, we had not been permitted to visit the churches and so, of course, had not come in contact with this custom. So we asked some of the elders about it. They replied that once a month they celebrated the Lord's Supper which they referred to as The Secret.

"Before the missionaries were evacuated from the country, they had gathered from time to time with the Christians to observe the Lord's Supper. They usually met in one of the homes on the mission station as the number of baptized believers was not great. In recalling the way we conducted this service, the Wallamo Christians somehow had gotten the idea that it was not to be done in the presence of unbelievers. We further learned that candidates for baptism would not be baptized until they had promised not to divulge what was taking place when they sat around the Lord's Table. We were somewhat amused to learn that although the unbaptized believers and unbelievers were dismissed from the service at the time of the serving of the Lord's Supper, they were invited to return at its conclusion to participate in the offering which followed."

When Walter Ohman asked the elders about this, they said, "Oh, this has always been our practice, we like it this way and we have no desire to change it." However, when a careful study of I Corinthians 11:23-27 was shared with them, they realized that they had misinterpreted the manner of conducting this service and realized that the observance of the Lord's Supper was actually intended to be a witness to unbelievers.

Other matters arose from night to night in these sessions. One evening, in discussing their experiences and the changes in their way of living, someone asked if there was anything against their herding goats. They told how they no longer kept goats, for they had read in the gospel of Matthew that the sheep and the goats were to be separated!

From these evening Bible studies the missionaries realized that the churches had pastors who knew little of what the Word of God taught, and that a Bible school was a priority need. Many of the pastors were completely illiterate. Some were preaching a message of legalism, while the church as a whole still fasted on Fridays.

At the same time, the missionaries learned of the monthly meetings of the church leaders for prayer and discussion of church problems, in an effort to overcome the lack of teaching. Elders chosen from the various districts of the provinces — by 1946 there were eight districts — were in charge. Each of the one hundred and fifty churches was allowed to send two representatives to the meetings which were held at different churches.

It was the fall of 1946 before permission was granted to move to the old mission station site at Otona. Since compensation for the expropriated properties had been paid to the S.I.M. by the Italian Government in 1937, all of the former mission properties rightfully belonged now to the Ethiopian government. A contract agreement was drawn up with the government for the use of the former mission properties on the promise that the mission would supply a doctor to run the hospital.

All of the buildings, however — the residences as well as the hospital rooms — were occupied by squatters along with their cattle and other animals. The men's ward had been used as a courtroom, and the judge had used the pantry as a stable, leaving the manure to accumulate into a four-foot pile. The Ohmans, joined by Dr. and Mrs. Nathan Barlow, had the right to occupy the property, but taking possession was another matter. It was a difficult task requiring great diplomacy to squeeze these unlawful residents from the buildings. But one by one, the rooms were taken over, cleaned out, refurbished, redecorated and locked.

At last in October it was possible to move into the buildings. And even before equipment could be ordered for the hospital, news of the doctor's arrival had gone out from Otona and patients were beginning to come for treatments.

16 ⁓ Food for the Body— Food for the Soul

Who, when he came, and had seen the grace of God, was glad, and exhorted them all, that with purpose of heart they would cleave unto the Lord.
— Acts 11:23

"ONE DAY one of the pastors came," reports Laurie Davison, "to ask if I would accompany him to a baptismal service out on the borders of the Wallamo area. I gladly went along, even though it wasn't a very good day. The length of the journey did not permit us to reach our destination that evening and so we stayed overnight en route.

"When we arrived next morning, hundreds of people were already gathered. This was my first experience back in the area and out among the churches, seeing things as they were. Arrangements had been made for a baptismal service to be conducted in a small creek about a half mile from the new church which was in the process of being built, and I went with the crowd to see what would happen. (I had been told that I would not speak at the baptismal service, but that they would like me to address the church later.) Two of the elders assisted the pastor, and they baptized sixty people. It took a

150

rather long time. Then we all returned to the church.

"What a joyful time it was! On the way to the baptismal service, the people had been fairly quiet. Now on the return journey everyone was shouting and singing. Somehow it seemed to touch off a deep spring in their hearts and release their feelings of unrestrained rejoicing.

"The church, we found, was a large round building only half constructed. The walls were there but no roof, only the cloudy sky above. It was a large building, as churches in Wallamo go, sufficient for several hundred people to be seated inside on the floor.

"As the service began, it started to rain. One of the believers ran quickly outside to a wild banana patch and plucked a large leaf. He returned and held it over my head while I stood before them, my New Testament opened, and shared with them the things concerning their new-found Lord and Master.

"The Lord visited us with unusual blessing that day, in spite of the rain and the canopy held over my head that rustled to and fro in the wind. The people made no move to go home. They simply sat there with the rain pelting down upon them, as I talked on and on to them from the Word of God.

"The rain at last subsided, and as it cleared, preparation was made for the Communion service. The Communion wine was made of honey mixed with water. The bread was the ordinary Wallamo kind of corn meal cake, broken up into small pieces and passed around among the people by the elders. Of course, the people were not sitting in rows, and the church was so full that the elders had to jump from place to place as they moved among the people. The drink was served in bottles of varying sizes and shapes, obviously made for other purposes. They went from person to person giving each a little sip and then passing on to the next one. Possibly

Jaldo, one of the first believers and a strong leader of the church.
Füssle

Typical Wallamo greeting. SIM

After Bible study, church leaders take a little food for the body—cornbread with meat gravy, washed down by honey water.
Niger-Challenge

A Wallamo communion service is very simple, using honey water in various sizes of containers and plain cornbread.
Füssle

Christians sit on the floor in their tiny church for the communion service. Füssle

to Western Christians it would seem to be very crude and primitive and far removed from the dignity of our church communion services. But to these people, it was a living experience of the presence and power of the Lord."

Not long after the baptismal service, Davison was asked to go to one of the leaders' monthly meetings. Each time the moon was full, the elders, evangelists and pastors of the churches would gather at a different church in a different part of the province. In the course of a year, they would cover quite a large area with their spiritual ministry. These monthly meetings were open to the general public for the first part of the session which amounted to a spiritual life conference.

The host church not only provided food for those who came, but saw to it that the travelers' feet were washed when they arrived at the church. This is a lovely Wallamo custom, deeply rooted in the culture and without any religious significance. The host church was also responsible for sleeping quarters. The men were usually bedded down on deep, freshly cut grass in the church, while the women visitors were looked after in nearby homes or separate quarters.

"This particular monthly meeting was out on the plains toward Lake Abaya, and it was necessary for us to travel by mule a day's journey to reach there," relates Laurie Davison. "I was quartered in a small home for the night adjacent to a large meeting house. People began to gather in the late evening after dark and kept on coming right through until morning. As the evening wore on, all began to sing. They shared testimonies and experiences, although there was no formal meeting until the next day. In the hut with me that night were the elders who had come for the monthly meeting. They had fixed a little platform of sticks for me to sleep on, while they slept on grass spread on the floor.

"Early the next morning I was awakened by soft talking. As I opened my eyes, I saw some of the men sitting up and talking together in whispers. I thought it would be interesting to see what they would do, and so I continued to appear to be sleeping. I could hear the women outside preparing something in the way of a meal — the breakfast menu usually consisted of roasted grain and coffee. I listened carefully to the elders and found they were discussing a matter of church government. Apparently, a couple had gotten into difficulty in their married life, and some form of discipline would have to be administered by the church in an official way. The men were discussing what should be included in the discipline and how it should be handled.

"The door of the hut must have been facing eastward. As the sun peered over the horizon, it shone directly in through the open door onto the little group. Of course, they were not fully dressed. Sitting here and there with trousers in hand, squatting on the grass scattered on the floor, slowly dressing, these men, church leaders all, were deeply engaged in discussing a most serious and far-reaching matter which could come before a church council.

"I smiled to myself as I thought of the dignity of similar gatherings held in the homeland. Here we had a man with his trousers off, examining them carefully for any possible livestock right in the center of the whole conference. It was quite new to me that God should work in this way. I marveled that God should be among these people, and that this group of men should be the Holy Spirit-filled leaders, working out the policies of the church under His guidance. Some, and perhaps most who read this story, will assume that church leaders in such a conference would be found in proper buildings with suitable tables and chairs with files and paper, the meeting conducted according to prescribed rules of order. But here in this faraway, hidden and unseen place, the Holy Spirit in all of His fullness was equally able to conduct the business of the church in circumstances that were equally proper to Him.

"Soon the roasted wheat and maise, together with the coffee, was brought in. I sat up in bed joining the group for our first meal of the day.

"Immediately after breakfast I was escorted to the church building, which by this time was absolutely packed with believers waiting to hear a message from God. What a privilege and what an opportunity it was to tell them the things that God had indicated were to be their spiritual food for this month! Then, the meeting over, the entire group broke up and with much rejoicing, hymn-singing and praise they melted away to their own particular spheres of service."

Walter Ohman vividly remembers one of the first monthly meetings he attended. It was held in Koisha at Cowna Gafato's church. Most of the visitors did not arrive until after dusk. About eight o'clock in the evening the meeting was started with prayer, followed by four songs and two speakers. As the service was concluded, small grass tables were brought in and everyone was served. By the time all had eaten, it was approximately eleven o'clock. Being very tired, he was looking forward to using the bed-roll that he had brought along — but it was in a hut with the eighteen elders. As he was preparing to retire he was informed by the elders that they were going to discuss some rather knotty problems and wanted him to meet with them. It was after midnight when they decided to adjourn for the night. Most of them had come from far distant places and were very tired. By 12:30 all were fast asleep, amid much snoring. After some time he too, fell asleep.

At 2:30 a.m. Gafato came in and awakened them saying it was time to eat. They had just eaten, it seemed to Walter, following the evening service, but now they were served again with a hearty full-sized meal, accompanied by the ever-present Wallamo coffee. Coffee grows throughout most of Ethiopia and is a national drink. Among the Wallamos it is served with rancid butter and salt — very tasty. By 3:30 they were asleep again, only to be awakened at 5:30 by singing which came from the church. This was the call to prayer. Soon many could be heard taking part in prayer. In the hut the elders were also kneeling before the Lord. At six o'clock with prayers concluded and much scurrying about, everyone washed up with water from huge water pots set at the rear of the church building. Another meeting of prayer and two messages followed, when all were fed again.

Thinking that they would now be leaving to return home, Walter began to gather his things together. However, he was informed that they had not finished all of the business. While most of the visitors did leave, there were groups still waiting for individuals to receive answers to their questions or problems. By ten o'clock the problems had been solved; coffee and parched corn were brought for them to eat before they left. Now, finally, they were on the way home. But a stop was necessary at a church which had prepared a meal for them! The elders of the church had insisted that since they would be returning home by the road that passed their church, the missionary and elders from Soddo must stop in for a rest and a meal.

Recalling a similar experience, Mr. Ohman relates: "One day Mrs. Ohman and I were on our way to one of these monthly meetings, this time in Oferi, northeast of Soddo. Jaldo, the elder who had come to lead the way as our guide, had arranged for several stops in churches on the way to the Oferi church. After being on the road about an hour and a half, we stopped at a church and were served sweet potatoes and coffee. The sweet potatoes were eaten, dipping them into a very hot pepper sauce. This was a pleasant break in the journey, and we were soon back in the saddle and on our way. About an hour later we again pulled up at a church. I was reluctant to stop again, anxious to get on and reach our meeting. When we were assured by the people that everything was ready and realizing that it would not be well to offend them in such a manner, we dismounted and ate with them. Having eaten not long before, we couldn't eat much of this and were soon on our animals again.

" 'How much farther to the church where the meeting is to be held?' I asked Jaldo after another hour of travel.

"Jaldo replied, 'Oh, not too far now.'

"About twenty minutes later we stopped in front of a little church, much too small to hold a meeting of all the elders, and I asked Jaldo if this was the church for the meeting.

"Grinning, Jaldo replied, 'No, but they have prepared some food for us here.'

"I'm afraid that was one of my bad moments. Another stop for eating was too much for me. 'I am not eating here,' I told them. 'In fact, I am not even getting off my animal. If you and the others want to eat, hurry up!'

" 'But you must eat, master, they have prepared this for you.' Jaldo implored me.

"Mrs. Ohman thought we had better go in, so as not to offend them, but I said 'I am not going to eat, I am going to teach them a lesson.'

"But instead, they taught me a lesson. The Wallamos had all gone into the church. I could hear them conferring together as to how they were going to get us to come in. Then Jaldo came out. 'Godo, you don't have to eat. Just come in and thank God for the food.'

"So what else could I do but go in? To please the woman who had prepared the food, I did nibble a bit, which seemed to make her very happy."

Although the Wallamos love to be hospitable and to offer their guests food, they do not spend all their time eating! Nor is food for the body the primary concern of the Christians. The church leaders particularly recognized the great need for organized Bible teaching, and with the missionaries began to pray about starting a Bible-training school.

When the missionaries took over the old station site at Soddo they inherited several good stone buildings erected by the Italians. These stone buildings were suitable for classrooms for both a Bible and an elementary school. However, since many of the pastors would have to come long distances, it would be necessary to have a dormitory as well. The missionaries discussed this with the church leaders who decided that they would all come in to give their time to the erection of such a building.

The building of the walls and the bringing in of the timbers was divided so that each of the eight church districts was responsible for so many feet of wall, so many timbers, and the mudding of these walls. The missionaries made themselves responsible for the putting on of the corrugated iron roofing which came from another unused Italian building.

Word was sent out that the school could accommodate sixty pastors for the first semester in 1946. But the elders said that there were many more pastors than that waiting to come and they would be willing to double up so that all could come. That would not be for the best, the missionaries pointed out, especially for healthy living conditions.

It was finally worked out that seventy-two students could come. They made their own mattresses and wooden beds, and paid a fee of three Ethiopian dollars a month, about U.S. $1.20. This fee provided the basic study facilities, papers and pencils, kerosene for their lamps, and one bar of soap per month for each man. The second term with added accommodation the school took in ninety-three and the third term more than a hundred.

17 ~ Bibles and Dreams

So mightily grew the word of God and prevailed.
— Acts 19:20

"WE COULD NEVER, never have stood the testing and persecution, the suffering of those years, if we hadn't had this little booklet, *God Hath Spoken*. Although we know it is only a small part of God's message, the Scripture verses in it were just what we needed when we had nothing else."

I looked at the tattered and torn eight-page pamphlet held reverently and carefully in Markina's brown hands. Even in 1964 this was a precious possession. The once white pages were now darkly stained with use. The edges of the pages were torn and frayed. In places the printing was almost illegible. To preserve the paper cover which had become detached I noted the entire booklet had been sewn by hand to a small patch of brown cloth which evidently came from someone's old coat or trousers. For many of the Wallamo Christians this was the Word of God — all they had in their own language and dialect. This was what God had used to sustain them; it was their bread of life in great hunger and privation.

161

Little wonder then that the few copies which they possessed were soiled and worn through constant usage. Since new copies were not available after the supply left with them was exhausted, they guarded their personal copies with their lives. Others who wanted copies of their own, resorted to handwritten copies which were by comparison much more costly.

The little pamphlet published by the Scripture Gift Mission was one thing which God used to help and sustain the Wallamo believers through the times of persecution during the Italian administration. It had been the first portion of the Word of God translated into their language and they looked upon it with great reverence. Its contents were selected Scripture verses, without comment. The booklets had been distributed freely by the missionaries in pre-Italian days.

Walter Ohman had also translated the Gospel of Mark into Gofa, a dialect which varies somewhat from regular Wallamo. But in the absence of a more suitable and understandable version the Gofa Mark was greatly treasured by the believers. The supply was very limited, and so it too was often laboriously copied out by hand — costing in this form a considerable sum of money.

Just before we were sent out of Wallamo, Walter Ohman was working on the translation of the gospel of John, but it was completed too late to be published and distributed before we left. However, as the country opened up again toward the end of World War II, some 900 copies were available. When the Wallamo believers came up to Addis Ababa to see the Davisons, they were overjoyed to learn that another book of the Bible was in the Wallamo tongue. The gospels of John were divided into packages of 40 pounds each, wrapped in cowhides as camouflage from thieves, as well as to make them water-proof, and carried as head loads to Wallamo.

The complete Bible in Amharic has always been available

to the Wallamos, and some of the Christians had copies. But because they knew so little Amharic, especially the vocabulary used in the Scriptures, they had a hard time reading and understanding it.

Soon after Ethiopia was reopened to missionary work, a regulation was made which required all literature printed and published in the country to be done in the Amharic language. The stated purpose of the regulation was to unify the country and peoples by the use of one official language. This imposed and still imposes a most difficult obstacle for the many non-Amharic-speaking peoples who want to read the Word of God in their own language. The regulation is still in force and means that the majority of the present adult generation may never have the Word of God in a language they completely understand. It is very hard to grow spiritually without a knowledge of the Scriptures.

In a generation or two this problem may largely disappear, since all education is in the Amharic language. The younger generations can learn to read and understand the Scriptures. But to the present adult generation who love the Word of God it is for all practical purposes denied.

Still, they have not let this hindrance daunt them. An Amharic Bible is still a prized possession, to be pored over, and every truth treasured. Those who cannot read have memorized what they have heard others read, and have passed it on. They have obeyed what they do know. And the Holy Spirit has proven able to meet their needs in this realm as in so many others. Where there is no written Word, God often reveals Himself to the one who seeks in other ways — through dreams and visions.

Just prior to being expelled from Wallamo, Walter Ohman and I went out to Koisha in western Wallamo province to

These were the first believers baptized by Walter Ohman and Ray Davis in Koisha in 1936. Sakala is on the right, Dana Gadaba next to him. Davis

Marcella Ohman, Selma Bergsten and Ray Davis look at a copy of God Hath Spoken. Füssle

This little booklet of Scripture verses, God Hath Spoken, *was the only Bible for many of the Wallamo believers during the war. This copy has seen constant use for at least 20 years.* Füssle

baptize a group of believers. The Word of God had been brought to this small family group by the missionaries who had traveled throughout the district on evangelistic tours. A number had believed and would walk from their village to the station at Soddo, a distance of twenty miles, one Sunday a month.

Among those baptized were two brothers, Maysabo and Sakala, their parents, and a minor chief, Dana Gadaba.

During the Italian occupation Sakala and his father were taken away by the authorities and were never heard from again. Maysabo was, even by Wallamo standards, a poor man, but he had a very beautiful daughter whose Christian character was just as lovely. A rich man wanted to marry her and offered an ox as a gift. But Maysabo refused. He said, "All I require of the one who marries my daughter is that he love her as much as I do. No gifts, thank you." When the daughter finally was married and received a gift of the thing she wanted most, it was a Bible.

Dana Gadaba was a wealthy chief. But he had never had the opportunity to learn to read, so his knowledge of the Bible came from what he heard. He memorized every Scripture verse that was read or quoted to him.

His wife was also a believer who delighted in telling everyone in the neighborhood about her new life in Jesus Christ. She would often tell her husband, "Now you leave the work of the house and field to me. I am strong, and with the help of the boys we can take care of everything. Your job is to go out and witness."

So Dana Gadaba became an evangelist. He roamed literally hundreds of miles over rugged terrain — mountains, deserts, swollen streams — in dry or rainy season. He was a unique character, simple in his faith and tireless in his witness for the Lord. When he found anyone who would listen he would

quote some of the Scripture he had memorized, and then begin
to preach. Often he would break off in the middle of his
preaching to sing a hymn or a chorus.

One of his favorite choruses that he sang and taught in
many places was:

> We want to go, we want to go,
> To that place where sorrow, sickness and death are no more,
> We want to go, we want to go.

Once he was called to the home of a man who had learned
the chorus at a meeting the night before. Dana Gadaba found
the man sick in bed. "Pray for me that I might be healed,"
the sick man asked.

With a twinkle in his eye, Dana Gadaba replied, "Why, only
last night you were singing, 'We want to go, we want to go.'
Now, when you are the least bit sick, you call me to pray
for you to be healed. I thought you wanted to go!"

Ginja and Walde were brothers-in-law who worked for the
missionaries at Soddo in the early days of the station there.
Both learned to read with the help of the Lewises for whom
Walde did the cooking. And both made a profession of faith
in Christ.

But after the missionaries left, Ginja began to do some self-
examining and became quite troubled. He had realized the
seriousness of not really acting on the Word of God which he
had heard, and which he said he believed.

"You and I have worked for the white man," Ginja said to
Walde, "and we have heard the Word of God. We have said
that we believed . . . but do we? Have we truly repented?"

As they thought over these things, Walde and Ginja decided
to spend a night by themselves in a small hut, to talk and
pray. That night they both determined to trust in Jesus Christ
and to follow and obey Him.

But Ginja was still distressed. He was constantly asking himself, "What will I say when I stand before the Lord?" One night he lay down to sleep, but though he was very tired, sleep would not come. Then it seemed as though a bright light appeared before him. He thought he heard a voice saying, "Ginja, you place your Bible in a clay pot and you just rest? You do not read my Word? Why have you hidden your Bible in that clay pot? I will ask you about that some day if you do not take it out and read it."

Frightened, Ginja went to Walde and said, "I am going to work for the Lord." God had been speaking to Walde as well, and the two of them resolved to give themselves entirely to God for His service. They began by witnessing everywhere they went. After a time Walde became a pastor of a large church not far from the mission station. When he died after many years of faithful service, Ginja was given the work of pastoring this church.

The power of the Word of God has always been graphically demonstrated among the Wallamo people. Though they possess only fragments, it has always been enough to meet their need. Perhaps the dynamic which is the essence of the Word of God, when mixed with the simple, wholehearted faith of the Wallamo believers, has been more fully released to fulfill its purpose.

18 ⌒ Healing and Prayer

*By stretching forth thine hand to heal; and that
signs and wonders may be done by the name of thy
holy child Jesus.*

— Acts 4:30

"LORD, YOU HAVE SAVED this man, and he is Your
child. Will You not also touch his eyes, that he may be able to
see — that he may be able to go about witnessing for You?"

The Wallamo church was praying in answer to a challenge.

One of the believers had been blind for sixteen years. In
meditating upon his salvation he concluded that if God was
able to change his life, would He not be able to give him back
his sight? He discussed the idea with his family and together
they brought the matter to the church elders. The leaders
assured the family that God could heal in answer to prayer, if
it was to His glory and according to His will.

In answer to the prayer of the believers, God did the miracle
that was necessary. The man's sight was completely restored.
But this was not the end of the remarkable story. Let the
once-blind believer tell it in his own words:

"After some months had passed, the newness of my salva-

168

tion and my restored eyesight became common to me. I could see the trees, the cows, the people. It happened that I was not praising the Lord as I had before — I was busy about one thing and another. Then, one day, when I was out on the path, I met some of my old companions — those with whom I had worked and with whom I had sacrificed to Satan in days past. They were sitting by the side of the road. They had killed an animal which they were sacrificing to Satan. Now, I had no part at all in the sacrifice. I just came along the path and sat down where they were sitting and watched them. I talked with them about the sacrifice which they had made but I myself had no part in it. I watched them as they carried on the sacrifice, even as I had in days past when I had been one with them.

"Then, all of a sudden my sight left me. It happened while I sat with those men as they were sacrificing to Satan. I returned immediately to the church and told the elders what had happened. I asked them to pray for me again. I confessed to them what I had done. I confessed that I had sat with those who were sacrificing to Satan, I had looked at the sacrifice, I had talked with them, that then, suddenly, the Lord had taken away my sight.

"I begged the elders saying, 'Will you pray the Lord to give me back my sight? Will you help me pray that I may again be able to see? That I may again see my family, my wife, my children, my home? Will you pray that the Lord will forgive me, and give me back again my eyesight?'

"The church prayed. They said to me, 'After you confess your sin to the Lord, we will help you pray.' So they prayed and prayed. Each time they met they prayed that I might receive my sight, as it had been before. They continued in prayer for many months, and at last the Lord gave me back my sight. It was not as sudden an answer to prayer as before, nor was the eyesight as clear as the first time. But the Lord gave me back my eyesight and I want to thank Him. I am unworthy of it, but I do praise the Lord for what He has done for me. Will you pray that I may go on walking with the Lord — that I may serve Him — that I may not go back into the old ways?"

Talgorei's story is another example of God's working in answer to prayer. Talgorei was 14 when she heard the Gospel and believed. She had never been able to walk because of some birth defect. When the time came for her baptism, she was carried on a litter into the stream, baptized, and carried out again.

That same day Talgorei's mother went to the church elders and asked them to pray for her daughter. She, too, reasoned that if God was able to give her daughter salvation, was He not able to heal her body and strengthen her? That night the church met to pray for Talgorei. They prayed, sang and read from the few Scripture portions they had. The next day Talgorei walked all the way from her home to the church — about five or six miles.

Other kinds of healing came in answer to the prayer of the Christians. About two years after the hospital was reopened in Soddo, some of the missionaries traveled out into the edges of Wallamo, doing evangelistic work and taking with them some medicine for the more common complaints and illnesses.

In one district the Christians had been urging a demon-possessed man to go to Soddo for medicine for his eyes, which were infected and giving him trouble. But he always refused.

"No, I cannot go to anyone who is talking about Jesus for medicine. I am worshiping Satan. I am possessed by Satan. I cannot go to those who are followers of Jesus."

But after a long period of sleepless nights with almost unbearable pain in his eyes, the Satan-worshiper gave in. He allowed himself to be brought on a mule to the local church where the missionary was staying.

The pastor and leaders of the church were elated. They had tried so hard to do something for this man, but he had always refused their kindnesses. But now he was actually coming. The pastor's house was prepared — fresh grass on the floor and a new mat.

While the missionary was putting drops in his eyes, some of the Christians cooked his food — the best food they could get. When he expressed gratitude for the relief from pain that came so quickly with the drops, the Christians prayed for him — in his presence — for healing physically and spiritually. "We want you to know the joy that we know," they told him.

That night the Satan-worshiper was able to sleep without pain. The next day the pastor invited him to stay on over the weekend so that he could attend a church service. When he heard the singing and saw the large group of happy people worshiping the Lord, his hard heart was softened. He stood to his feet and told the congregation, "I have rejected Jesus Christ for a long time, but today I want to follow Him. I thought I would never see again. I thought I would never want to follow the Lord as you people do."

The man went home to tell his family and village that he had become a true follower of the Lord. His wife had prayed for him for many months — she was already a believer.

But after some months, Satan seemed to say to him one Sunday, "Why did you go to church today?"

Again the next day the voice of Satan came. "Why did you go to church yesterday? Why did you go to that woman for medicine for your eyes, while I was making you blind? Don't you know that I am the one who took both of your children in one day? Don't you know that I am the one who destroyed your house — burned it with fire? How dare you stand against me? Don't you know that I have power? Don't you know that I am the one who caused you to fall and get hurt when you went into the church? Don't you know that I have power to do whatever I want?

"Now in order to get rid of that thing which you have done, sacrifice a white ox. You must sacrifice him immediately. There must be new blood to cleanse you now from what you have done — going into the church and saying that you have accepted Jesus Christ as your Saviour."

For several days the evil voice continued to speak to him. He felt as though he were being beaten with rods which were pounding him to the ground. All his physical strength left him and he seemed almost dead, unable to move.

The church spent a great deal of time praying for him, and though the struggle was great, he was eventually delivered and strengthened. When he could walk again, he came to the church to give praise to the Lord for this new deliverance. This time there was no doubt that he had definitely given up Satan's ways and was following Jesus. Anyone listening to his testimony and his plea for continued prayer could not question it.

"I am through, I am through with Satan. I will be strong in the Lord. I believe in Him. Pray for me. Continue praying for me. Satan is going to trouble me, but keep on praying. I cannot stand against him unless you pray for me. I know the Lord is going to keep me."

He was questioned as to how it happened that he was troubled again, after he seemed to have come through in a true decision to follow Christ. His answer was, "I had stopped smoking, but I thought, *Surely there is no wrong in smoking and raising my own tobacco. I can do some of these things that*

I have done before. Surely, I don't have to give up everything.
So I filled my pipe and I smoked, enjoying it very much. I also
joined my former companions, and I went to them this particular afternoon. I went back into some of the things that I had
done before. Then it was the evil spirits came and troubled me.

"I confess that I did wrong, I confess that I sinned, I confess that I went after the old things of this life — the way that
I used to go — and I want the Lord to forgive me. I realize
now that I have done many other things, and I know Satan is
trying to get me to go back into my old practices. Satan was
the one who troubled me, and I yielded to him. This is why
I had trouble the second time."

In order to make his decision clear cut, he asked the elders
of the church to come and help remove the things in his house
that he had been using for Satan-worship. But before the
elders had time to reach his house, he himself had taken out
all of the articles and piled them outside. On the pile he also
put his pipe and tobacco. Then he went to the garden behind
the house and pulled up all his tobacco plants and put them
on the pile.

"Now, I am through with all of this," he said. "I don't
want anything more to do with it."

From then on, he gathered his wife and children for daily
prayer, asking the Lord to keep them strong and true. Today
this man is still standing firm, still following the Lord rather
than Satan.

Less spectacular "miracles" of healing occur from day to
day in the hospital at Soddo where Dr. and Mrs. Nathan Barlow
and others have been working since 1946. Some of the opera-
tions performed in the hospital have been dramatic enough —
tumors removed large enough to fill a water bucket or weighing
as much as the patient, emergency tracheotomies done in des-

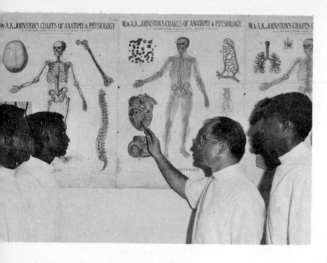

Part of the dresser-training program involves studying anatomy. Scheel

Below, Dr. and Mrs. Scheel and a dresser apply a plaster cast. Scheel

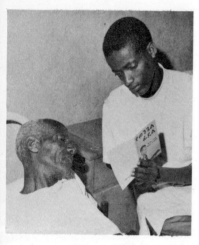

Above, a young Wallamo dresser helps an elderly patient learn the Amharic language. Scheel

A patient arrives at the Soddo hospital on a homemade stretcher carried by his friends. Scheel

peration with the doctor away. But as in most hospitals, the majority of cases tend to be the more "ordinary" kinds of illnesses. Others involve hours of poring over test tubes and microscope trying to match symptoms with disease — as in the recent outbreak of yellow fever in Southern Ethiopia. Yet no case is really ordinary, each is prayed over, and every treatment given is as much part of the story of Jesus' love as the more miraculous answers to prayer.

Many of the patients at the hospital hear about Jesus Christ for the first time, and many have believed and found a new way of life with "peace in their stomachs" as they put it. Missionary personnel do not do all of the talking either. A nurse on her rounds one day overheard this conversation between two patients.

"I have not much chance to hear the Gospel," one woman was complaining. "Out in my area there is no church. There are no believers."

"Suppose you were going to market," the other replied. "What would you consider far? You would not think it too far to go all the way to Bolosso, and buy something there. Then you would take it down to Dolo and sell it there to make a shilling profit. Why should you consider it a hardship to walk an hour or two to hear God's Word? Isn't God's Word worth more than what you can get in the market?"

When the Barlows first came to the hospital, they dreamed of providing medical training for Wallamo young people. Eventually the dream became a reality in the Dresser's Training School. Three years of study provide both theoretical and practical knowledge with the aim of graduating competent medical evangelists. Scientific techniques of modern medicine are stressed, but so is the necessity of an open and obedient Christian life. Graduate dressers have gone out from Soddo into all areas of Wallamo, and to other parts of Ethiopia.

19 ～ The Church in Action

. . . in a great trial of affliction the abundance of their joy and their deep poverty abounded into the riches of their liberality.

— II Corinthians 8:2

"WHEN YOU STAND in God's presence, *What will you say?*"

If you have not supported the ones whom He has sent,
What will you say?
If you have not made right the wrong you have done,
What will you say?

More than four thousand Christians, seated on the grassy slope under the eucalyptus canopy at Otona, were singing about their responsibility to obey God.

If you have not stopped your lying . . .
If you have not stopped your gossip . . .
If you have not stopped your anger . . .
If you have not done His will . . .
If you have not told to others the Gospel . . .
What will you say?

Looking out over the crowd from the platform at the lower end of the slope, one could see only a mass of brown faces, each one framed in white — the filmy shamma (shawl) that everyone wears about the shoulders, made of coarsely woven soft cotton tipped with colored fringes.

176

The morning sunlight filtered through the eucalyptus leaves and glinted off the women's colorful nylon nets that kept their bushy hair in place. White teeth flashed as the people answered the song leader:

> *What will He say?*
> When those who have never heard stand before **Him**,
> *What will He say?*
> When those who wanted to go to people in darkness
>   come and you did not encourage them,
> *What will He say?*

While the people sang, the elders picked their way through the tightly packed crowd, stepping over one, around another, turning here and there in no apparent order. Hands reached up to put things in the elders' hats or over their arms: coins of various sizes, produce, coats, shawls, sweaters, scarves, shoes, boots. Here and there someone stood up to take off a piece of clothing to give for the offering.

When the singing stopped, the elders piled all the gifts on the platform and returned to their seats on either side of the platform facing the congregation. After the service was over they would count the cash. The other things would eventually be sold in the market and the amount added to the total offering.

This was the annual Bible conference, the high point of the Wallamo church year. Every Christian who could get away from his work was here, even if only for a day or two of the week of meetings. The day had begun with an hour of prayer before daylight. This service had started at nine, and there would be a second speaker after the offering. Then the noon meal, then another service like this one. The evening meeting would be especially for the non-Christians who found the crowds and the activity something of a spectacle. Films, slides, evangelistic messages would stress the meaning and importance of Jesus Christ's life and death.

A hush settled over the congregation as the second speaker

began his message. They listened eagerly to every word, not wanting to miss any of the important truths they were hearing. This privilege of having special speakers from outside of Wallamo came infrequently.

When the speaker closed his message with a call for volunteers to take the Gospel to unreached areas, more than 100 stood quietly to their feet. There was no great emotion, but a dignified and solemn act of commitment to Jesus Christ for His service.

The first Bible conference was held in November, 1948. The idea came as the answer to a great many problems. Most of the believers knew little of what the Bible taught, and few of the church leaders had had much Bible teaching in depth. Nor had all the Wallamo Christians ever gotten together in one place — something that could give them the consciousness of solidarity and oneness.

The idea was received enthusiastically by the church leaders. It posed difficulties, however. No one could foresee how many would come to such a conference, or how long they would stay if they did come. Some of the elders thought perhaps as many as a thousand would come; others, more optimistic, predicted up to two thousand. But where could such a crowd meet? No building on the mission station could hold that many, even with Wallamo crowding.

November was dry season, though, so the services could be held outdoors. A grassy slope between the two Bible school buildings would be just the place, and with a temporary platform at the lower end everyone could sit comfortably on the ground and see as well as hear the speakers.

Protection from the hot noonday sun could come from a temporary arbor, made from eucalyptus poles tied together in a kind of overhead lattice work and covered with the leafy branches to provide aromatic shade.

Four thousand came to the first conference, to everyone's surprise. Some had to leave after two or three days, so that others would be freed to attend. (Wallamo life is such that with no locks on their doors, someone must always be present to guard the house and possessions against thieves, especially at night, and to look after the cattle.) The attendance stayed around 2500 during the rest of the week, and rose to 6,000 on the closing Sunday. Each person brought his own food with him.

Mr. Playfair was back again in Wallamo after his first visit five years before, and was the principal speaker. He brought a strong missionary challenge, presenting the need of the surrounding areas among the Wallamos and neighboring tribes. Forty young men responded to the challenge. When they were encouraged to come to Bible school, they all enrolled for that year.

At the 1949 conference the Christians were challenged to give their money to support these 40 young men who were ready now to leave home and preach the Gospel. By the end of the conference, the gifts amounted to $368 Ethiopian dollars ($150 U.S.) — the first offering contributed by the Wallamo church as a whole and at one time.

"We have become like white people in giving." This was the Christians' reaction when they learned that their conference gifts in 1950 had increased to $1800 Ethiopian dollars ($720 U.S.). Most of them counted their own money in pennies. They had also taken quite a step of faith. Reminded again of their responsibility to the many Wallamos and others who hadn't heard about Jesus Christ, they promised that from then on, half of all the local church offerings would go to support evangelists.

Although the Wallamos are a poor people by Western standards, they were not satisfied to keep their giving at the

Instead of a car park, a mule park! Conference visitors leave their transportation tied up to rest. Niger-Challenge

Conference offerings come not only in cash but in clothing which will later be sold. Füssle

Cotton spun into thread will earn a few cents at the nearest market — or else be woven into cloth for a shawl or dress. Füssle

Thousands of Christians attend the Soddo conference every year, crowding under the eucalyptus canopy to hear the Word of God. Füssle

same level. Their joy in Christ and their love increased their desire to share what they had and to give for the sake of others. But they had virtually no ready cash or even tangible assets. At the next Bible conference, a few Christians stood up in one meeting to promise that they would give a certain amount to the Lord during the next year. They would trust Him to give them enough money to keep that promise.

The idea immediately caught fire. Christians stood by the score to make similar faith promises — a sheep, a donkey, a horse, a blanket, ten dollars, the produce of ten coffee trees. These promises were not made lightly but as a serious obligation between the individual and the Lord. Still there was a kind of holy hilarity at being able to give so much out of love for Jesus Christ. The total gifts and promises came to 5200 Ethiopian dollars ($2100 U.S.).

During the following year each one worked hard to pay the promise in full, often in small installments. By the next conference, a careful check showed that every penny promised had been paid.

Since that first year, the challenge of this kind of giving has grown. Perhaps it seems strange to us, who see the Wallamos as among the "have-nots" of the world. The Wallamo way of life, as for most of the world's peoples, is concerned mainly with the provision of the physical needs. Even the few wealthy Wallamos have very little by Western standards. The Wallamos "enjoy" life, but it is not easy, convenient or affluent. Nor has becoming a Christian changed that aspect of life. The Christians do not find it easy to pay their faith-promises, but they seldom let the payments fall. Sometimes a wife or husband will take an unpaid promise as his or her own, if the other has died without being able to complete it. And often, payment takes longer than one year.

A man came into the bookshop in Soddo one day, quite

weary and hardly able to stand up. Selma Bergsten offered him a chair and he dropped onto it, murmuring repeatedly, "Thank You, Lord, for letting me come." Finally he told his story.

He was a poor man. In order to earn a little more money he had left his wife and family and gone into the Dorsey District quite a distance away, and gotten work as a weaver. There he was able to earn a cloth for his wife, one for himself, and enough money to pay his faith promise.

From his coat pocket he pulled out a small cloth bag, and put the money into Miss Bergsten's hand. When she checked the faith-promise book, where the pledge had been recorded, she found that it was five years since the man had made his promise. After she had recorded the payment in the book, and put the money away, the man sighed deeply and said, "Already I am beginning to feel better and stronger. I have been praying for months that the Lord would allow me to live until I was able to pay up my promise."

Today the receiving and recording of promises at the Bible conference is well organized. At the end of each morning and afternoon service (both about three hours long), people who want to make faith-promises stand up to give the details to elders or teachers who are stationed around the congregation. Name, district, and kind of gift are recorded for accuracy's sake, but everyone is aware that the promise is voluntary, made to God not to man. The Wallamos have no banking facilities, so the records and the monies are kept with the missionaries.

The Bible conference offerings and promises are not the only opportunities for giving. Regular tithes and offerings are taken up every Sunday in the local churches, and according to the promise made at the second annual conference, divided in half — half for the local church and half for missionary and evangelistic work. Every month the missionary half is taken

A Wallamo woman. Füssle

to the elders' district meeting and put in the common treasury.

Every Thursday morning at the regular prayer meeting, the people give an offering for the care of the poor. The offering on the monthly Communion Sunday goes to the pastor, and may include grain, sweet potatoes, butter, clothing, besides cash.

Whenever the women have special Bible study meetings, they too give offerings, although they have very little they can call their own.

A week of women's meetings was just ending, and the women were beginning to leave for their homes, when Selma Bergsten noticed an older woman running up the road toward her as fast as she could. When she got to the top of the hill she was covered with perspiration and so out of breath she couldn't speak. Finally she gasped, "Oh, thank You Lord! Oh, thank You for bringing me here in time."

"It seemed very strange to me," Selma Bergsten recalls, "since it was quite obvious that she was not on time. I was amused, too, and asked her, 'Would you mind telling me why you say over and over again that you are thankful the Lord has brought you here in time?'

" 'Oh, Thank You Lord!' she said again. Then she fumbled with a string tied to her belt. 'I have been here in the women's classes all week. As you read to us from the Word of God and helped us to know what God has done for us, I wanted so much to have something to give to Him. Other women were making their gifts, but I had nothing to offer.

" 'But I did have a few pennies. So I took them and bought some cotton in the market. Every night I sat up late spinning the cotton into thread. I could not spin in the daytime because we were in class. Late last night I finished my spinning.

" 'This morning I rose early, long before daylight, and walked to market.'

"That market was nearly five hours' walk away. There she bartered and sold the thread she had spun, and started back to Soddo. All the way she was praying 'Lord, help me to get back there in time to make my offering.'

" 'Look,' she said to me, 'God told me to give this money, and He brought me here in time to give my offering to Him.'

"Opening her hand she placed in mine the equivalent of eight U.S. cents."

PART VII
LIVING FLAMES

20 — Nana

And they departed from the presence of the council, rejoicing that they were counted worthy to suffer shame for his name. And daily in the temple, and in every house, they ceased not to teach and preach Jesus Christ.

— Acts 5:41, 42

"WELL, DO YOU THINK you want him?" the elder asked the missionary. Then he turned to Nana.

"Go out now. We will talk together whether we want you or not."

"I think he looks sleepy and drowsy," said the missionary when the tall, thin young man had left. "I don't know if he will be quick in his work or not."

The elder laughed, "Don't be concerned about his being sleepy. He has come a long way today and is tired from the hot sun. He will do all right. If that is the only thing you object to, try him." So it was agreed, and Nana came to work in the missionary's house.

Nana actually did much better than was anticipated and the missionaries were pleased to find that he could read. He had worked for them several months before they heard his story. He told it to them one evening at their request. As a young child, he had come to know the Lord through the witness of the believers in his area, particularly through the elder who had brought him in for work.

When he first believed, Nana said, his elder brother also believed but was not very strong in the Lord. Nana, however, had seen in the elder a life that was strong and true, as well as joyful, and he wanted to follow the Lord and become like this elder. He faithfully attended the services in his church, especially the early morning prayer meetings on Thursdays. Nana had a long way to reach the church and his parents were not at all in favor of his going to the services. They tried every possible way to discourage him. Often when he got up on Thursday morning, he would find that his cloth had been hidden so that he could not go.

One day his mother told him that not only would his cloth be taken away, but that she would not prepare any food for him on Thursdays or Sundays if he was going to church. That did not stop Nana. *That's not so bad*, he thought, *to miss my meals one day in order to hear the Word of God. Surely that is not too great a punishment.* But he did not know what to do about his clothing. When he told some of the people in the church about it, they arranged to provide him another cloth wrap. He would wear it in church and then leave it in a neighbor's home until the next service.

On other days, when meals were provided for him in his parent's home, he wanted to ask the blessing before he ate, but he was not allowed to do so. His parents said, "You're not going to pray at our meal-time. We don't believe as you do, and you can't do that in this house."

But Nana said to himself, "How can I eat without giving thanks — without thanking God for giving me food to eat?"

He finally decided to start scratching his ankles before he ate. His mother thought that it must be that his ankles were sore. She didn't know that as he scratched and looked at his ankles he closed his eyes and thanked the Lord for his food.

When he wanted to have a time of prayer, Nana would go out into the cornfield. There he had wonderful times together with the Lord on his knees.

Nana's father and mother were perplexed as to how they could stop their boy from believing in this new faith that had been brought in by the white people. Perhaps, they thought, if he was separated from other Christians he might change. So they went to the Italians and asked them to take Nana down into the lowlands and give him work in the cotton fields. "Do anything you want to do with him," they said, "but keep him there. Don't let him come back. Give him work, and make him work hard." The Italians were glad to take Nana for they needed healthy young workers in the cotton fields.

Nana had heard many stories of the difficulties others had experienced in the cotton fields. Fearful of what lay before him, he asked the Lord to keep him well physically. He felt that in fellowship with the Lord he could go on indefinitely, but if he got sick he hardly knew what would happen. There was much malaria in the lowlands. Since he thought that malaria came from water, he asked God to keep him from ever getting thirsty.

"You know," he said, "not once did I get thirsty down in the lowlands. I was just rejoicing in the Lord. Finally, there was an opportunity one day and so I ran away."

Although his parents were not too happy to see him, Nana was glad to be back. At his first opportunity he went to the church, glad to be back with his friends again.

About this time his mother became ill. Nana stayed at home and cared for her for quite some time, doing all he could to help. Then one Wednesday night his mother died. Nana was not at all happy at the thought of missing the Thursday morning prayer meeting, so before dawn, as usual, he slipped out of the house and went to the church.

At the prayer meeting the believers were asked to go to the funeral to encourage and help Nana. When they arrived at his home, they saw that large crowds of people had already gathered, for the burial was to take place late that afternoon. Nana took his place in the family group, and though he showed sorrow at his mother's death he did not wail or scratch his face or tear himself as the other members of the family did. But some of the older men were angry and threatened him, saying that if he did not enter into the proper weeping and wailing as they had always done, something fearful would happen to him.

Nana replied, "I cannot do what you are doing and dishonor my Lord. I know Jesus Christ is my Saviour and He has given me joy, even at a time like this."

Again they threatened Nana. Still he refused to weep and wail. So the men grabbed him, put a rope around the back of his neck, forward over his arms and down around his back and pulled him up to an overhanging branch in a tree. There they let him hang.

It was not too difficult at first.

He thought, *I can take this rather than bring reproach on my Lord.* But they left him hanging from the limb until late afternoon.

"By that time," he said, "I felt that my body was so heavy. The rope was cutting me, making deep marks in my body. Even though it hurt terribly, that did not seem too much. While I was hanging from the limb of the tree, I realized that there was nothing to stop me talking to the Lord. The Lord talked to me, and gave me great joy, gave me strength to bear the pain. There wasn't anything I lacked just because I was in that position."

Toward evening the father said, "If my son is going to leave me altogether like this and follow another faith, there is no need of having him punished longer. He won't give in now any more. I will send him out to herd the cows, to bring them home at dark." (To be sent out for the cows after dark is a great disgrace to anyone in a family where there is a funeral.)

"I was glad to go out and herd the cows," was Nana's reaction. "There I could talk to Jesus and ask Him to speak to my people, to make me strong for Him."

For the next several years Nana lived at home with his father. Now he had come to the mission to secure work so he could find money for food and clothing, which he greatly needed.

He had not been in the missionary's home too long, when he came one day and said, "I don't think I can work here very much longer. The Lord is going to send me out to tell the Gospel to some who really need it."

"If the Lord is calling you to go out, then, of course, you must go. You need not work here any longer," the missionary replied, and encouraged him to go without delay. Nana decided that in less than two weeks he should leave to go out to preach.

But near the end of the two weeks Nana said, "I don't believe I will go just yet. I need some trousers. I have to get some more clothes. I can't go out with just this one suit of clothes. I think I will wait for a while and get some more money."

The missionary cautioned, "If the Lord is calling you, there is no point in staying around and trying to get some more clothes. The Lord will take care of the clothes part." So with this encouragement, Nana left.

Quite a distance beyond his home a church had been started but had as yet no pastor. To this church with its handful of believers Nana was appointed pastor. He preached on Sundays and Thursdays. On weekday mornings he held classes for pupils to learn to read. Not one in that little group had a Bible or a New Testament, because none could read. All were new Christians with everything to learn. Nana was in his element now — he had complete freedom all day long to give out the Word of God and teach the people to read it.

After some time, enemies of the Gospel came out and burned the church. Nana and the elders said, "It cannot be that this should stop us preaching. It must be that the Lord just wants us to have a bigger church." So the people rallied around Nana to build a larger church. More people came to the services, and the Lord blessed His Word. Many more were saved, and the small group grew in numbers week by week.

After Nana had been preaching for some time in this church, he arose one Sunday morning and asked, "How many Bibles and New Testaments are there this morning? Twelve Bibles and New Testaments. That's good! Since there are twelve of you who have Bibles or New Testaments and can read, the work is now yours. I believe the Lord is calling me to go out to another area where they have never before heard the Gospel."

But the believers disagreed. "Oh, no. We can never let you go. How can we go on with the Lord if you don't stay right here and shepherd us through the years ahead? What do you mean just leaving us like this? Do you want us to go back into the old life?"

"No, not at all, but now it is up to you to work. Until now you have been fed. Now you are to work. I feel that the Lord is calling me. It is His will for me to go and for you to take on the work that you can do here."

However the opposition to his going was so great that he stayed on for a while, not wanting to do injury to the work by leaving the Christians too quickly. He was a good pastor and a good preacher, patient and always seeking to help the people around him.

Then the time came when he went to the elders of the church. "Now I *must* go," he said. "The Lord will give you a pastor who will care for the work here in a good way. If you let me go and support me and pray for me, the Lord will bless your church even more than He has blessed us to this day."

Still the church was unwilling, but he continued trying to convince them. Eventually the church realized the missionary opportunity, and agreed for him to serve elsewhere than in their own little church.

"All right, we will let you go, and we will pray that the Lord will give us a new leader in our church."

By this time Nana had a wife and child. So the church said to him, "Now that you are going out, don't take your wife and child with you. Find a place where you can locate. We will take care of your wife and child until you return to take them to the work where the Lord is leading you."

It is men like Nana who have helped the growth of the church in Wallamo, men who would not be silenced by either persecution or comfortable security, but who continually told others about the good news of God's salvation. In Nana's story we can also see the continued reproduction and growth of the living seed that Jesus pictured in His parables — the local church growing, sending out new shoots, new seed, to reproduce itself again and again.

21 ⟶ Balotei

And a certain woman . . . which worshipped God, heard us: whose heart the Lord opened, that she attended unto the things which were spoken . . . .
— Acts 16:14

Balotei was among the first girls who learned to read and write in Wallamo. She came to know the Lord during the Italian occupation. Highly efficient in whatever she set her hand to do, Balotei was anxious to share her new-found joy and peace in salvation with other women. After the war was over she was one of five or six women who accompanied Selma Bergsten on her visits to the various churches conducting women's classes.

In her own home church a young man, Omochi, was very much interested in Balotei. As a small boy he had been herding the cattle one day, and had crawled into a little hole in the ground to get some protection from the wind. But a leopard had come along and had bitten him on the cheek. When the wound healed he was left with a great jagged scar under his right eye. He was a fine steady boy, rather quiet, while Balotei was the vivacious type. After the proper negotiations they were married, and Omochi began to preach at different places in Wallamo.

Their first child was a girl. She was one of the loveliest and prettiest little girls in the village. Balotei and little Persis were inseparable. Balotei talked to her child as though she understood everything she said. She told her of her problems as well as her joys. Balotei had a small unbleached cotton bag in which she carried her knitting and her notebook, with her name "Balotei" embroidered on the outside. Persis also had a similar little bag with her name on it, for carrying the things important to a three-year-old. Wherever Balotei went, there was Persis — even in the Women's Bible classes.

Then one day little Persis became ill. Balotei was expecting another child and could not take her to the hospital. Omochi was away preaching. So friends carried the child to the mission hospital at Soddo. But nothing could be done for her — and she died.

"How will Balotei ever take this?" was the question on everyone's mind — "her little Persis — they were so close." The friends who had brought Persis to the hospital wrapped the little body in a cloth and carried it back the two hours' walk to Balotei.

The next day Selma Bergsten followed the same path. What could she say, she wondered, to comfort this young mother? She asked God to give her something from His Word. Balotei was standing in the doorway as she walked down the path to the house. After the greetings they went inside to talk. Before the missionary could even begin to bring any comfort, Balotei exclaimed, "Isn't it wonderful! To think that my little girl is with the Lord! She was here just last week and today she is with the Lord! Isn't that wonderful! To think that the Lord should choose my girl, when there are so many lovely little girls! Yet the Lord chose mine! Isn't that wonderful!"

Here was no sorrow, only jubilation and amazement that the Lord had honored her by taking her little girl home to be with Himself. There was no thought of weeping sadly because her little girl was gone, only triumph.

Omochi heard the news of Persis' illness and started home the night she was taken to the hospital. He arrived just after the little body had been returned home — in time for the burial.

After Persis' death, Desita was born. He was quite different from Persis, very quiet, not at all vivacious. But Balotei was just as enthralled with Desita as she had been with Persis.

About this time Balotei and her husband realized that God was calling them to Gofa to preach the Gospel. Gofa was about two weeks' walk south and west. Omochi went ahead to search out the place where they could locate and build a house. He found a part of the tribe that had not been reached by anyone. There he chose a lovely spot on the side of a hill, built a house and planted a garden. Then he returned for Balotei and Desita, arriving shortly before the time of the annual conference.

Conference over, the day came when they were to leave. Another evangelist and his wife were starting off at the same time for the same general area. The two couples had decided to get a donkey together and load it so that they would not have to carry the grain they needed along the way. All of the provisions for the two couples were loaded on the one small donkey. Balotei carried a little clay pot with clabber milk in one hand and a small gourd with ground wheat in the other. Desita was strapped to her back. Omochi drove the donkey and the cow before them.

Thus they left home, turning their backs upon all that it means to have good neighbors to help, to have a market nearby where you can buy butter and salt. They left their fragile

native frying pan on which they roasted their grain, their
water pots, their home, their little plot of ground — everything
they had apart from their cow. Though these things were not
worth much perhaps in monetary value, leaving them repre-
sented a tremendous sacrifice. But they rejoiced in the privilege of leaving all their conveniences in Wallamo to go off to
Gofa, to make Christ known to people who had never heard
the Gospel.

It took them two weeks to reach their destination, due to
the slow pace of the animals and the baby on Balotei's back.
All the way they traveled on foot, up over stony mountains,
across streams which were sometimes deep and difficult to
cross, through wilderness areas, dangerous places where wild
animals and bandits lurked. They could not go too slowly
because there were wide rivers to ford before the rains became
too heavy and filled the rivers. At last they arrived in Gofa, and
Balotei was delighted with the little house and garden her
husband had prepared for them.

They had been there only three weeks when it became
necessary for Omochi to return to Soddo to care for a matter
of business. Balotei was not afraid to stay alone. She would
carry on in her husband's absence. She had already made
friends with the women and children. She would have reading
classes and also tell them about the Lord. Time would pass
quickly if she kept busy, and soon her husband would return.
Traveling alone back to Wallamo he was able to go much more
quickly, taking just over a week.

"When he reached Soddo, he came to my home," recalls
Selma Bergsten, "and we had coffee together. When I asked
about Balotei, Omochi said, 'Oh, she is all right. She will
carry on meetings and things like that until I come back.' He
also said that Balotei was very friendly with the neighbors,
which she naturally would be. She could keep a conversation

going when no one else could, and make it interesting too. He told me what day he was planning to return to see me. We waited for that day."

The morning Omochi was expected back, a messenger came with the word that he had been killed by a roving band of brigands.

Again the questions came. Balotei was alone in Gofa, two weeks' journey away, with her little Desita. How would she react to this news when the messenger came? There were no Christians anywhere around, no one to comfort her. What would she do? Who would be there to strengthen her when she heard that Omochi was not coming back?

The elders of the church at Soddo found a messenger to go to Balotei with the sad news. But God had already prepared her for the news.

One night not long after Omochi left, Balotei was awakened by a voice speaking to her. "Balotei," the voice said, "what would you do if your husband did not return?"

Balotei answered, "Of course he'll return. Lord, You brought us here to work for You and my husband hasn't been able to do much preaching yet—of course, he'll return." Balotei lay down to sleep again.

Once more she was awakened by a voice speaking to her, "Balotei, what would you do if your husband did not return?"

She hesitated for just a little while, and then said, "Well, Lord, if it is You who is talking, he is Yours and I am Yours. I guess You can do what You want with Your own." With that she lay down again but not to sleep. She kept thinking and wondering what this might mean.

From then on she began to look every day to see just who would be coming. She would wonder, *The day for his return is past.* But days went by. There was no word. Still he didn't come back.

Then one day, she recognized a man coming down the path, a man from her home district in Wallamo. She realized at once that it must have been true what the Voice had said to her. So, when she saw the man coming, she hesitated a moment. Then she started toward him calling, "Isn't he coming?"

The messenger replied, "No, he is not coming."

Hearing that, Balotei went back into her grass hut. She knelt down and asked the Lord to guide her as to what she should do. "If he is not coming back, Lord," she prayed, "then you will just have to guide me that much more."

There was no time to think further. Suddenly it seemed as though the whole neighborhood began to weep and wail. The weeping and wailing in that area of Gofa is most intense and severe. When the people are mourning, they jump high in the air and throw themselves to the ground, hitting its hard surface with a terrific thud. One wonders how a person can survive such severe knockings.

As each group came to weep and to show their sympathy, Balotei would go out to the people. "Why are you weeping?" she would ask. "Why are you wailing?"

"Oh, because your husband has been killed! Because your husband has been killed! Of course, we are weeping and wailing for him."

"Why do you do that? Why do you weep for my husband?"

"Because he isn't coming back," they cried.

"But I have told you ever since he went away of One who died for you. That One is Jesus Christ. Not once have you wept because of His death for you. Why do you weep for my husband? He didn't die for you. Jesus Christ died for you."

Then Balotei would explain again what Jesus Christ had done for them, and how if they would accept Him as their Saviour they, too, would be saved.

For all the days of customary mourning Balotei was strengthened to meet each group as they came to express their sympathy. Messages were sent down to her in Gofa from the elders of Soddo, saying, "You do not have to stay in Gofa now. You are all alone. You can come back. There is lots of work to do right here at home." But Balotei replied, "Why should I go back? When the Lord called by husband, He called me too, and I am going to stay here until He tells me to leave. The Lord has called me. I am going to stay."

Balotei stayed on until it was possible for the evangelists who were working elsewhere in the Gofa region to find someone to take over her work. She gathered the people through the week to teach them in one way and another, carrying on the work alone.

When the evangelist and his wife came to take over, Balotei was free to travel about and work among women and girls in the Gofa area. Other evangelists and their wives often called her to come into their areas where the people had responded and had come to know the Lord. She would hold two-week classes among the women and girls, just as the missionaries had done back in Soddo. As the work grew and the Christians increased, the churches asked her to stay longer — two months at a time.

As Balotei traveled from church to church, she continued to care for her little son Desita. Trudging over the rocky pathway, gourd in one hand, the wheat flour and the clay pot in the other, she carried Desita strapped on her back. When the new evangelist and his wife arrived to take over the work, Balotei moved out of the house Omochi had built for her. Never since then has she had a home of her own. She has no hut of which she can say, "This is my home, this is my bed, this is the place where I am going to stay for awhile."

She travels from group to group, teaching the women and children. Gathering as many as fifty children together in the

Balotei and Desita. Füssle

Marcella Ohman, Ray Davis, Selma Bergsten visit Balotei's home to hear her story. Füssle

Teaching women and children in their homes. SIM— K. Lovering

early morning before the cows are put out for grazing, she releases them when the time for their chores arrives. The children go home and the women come to have their classes throughout the day until the evening hours. Often in the evening, men and women come for the study of the alphabet, in order to learn to read their Bibles.

At the annual conference in Soddo following Omochi's death, Balotei was present. When she told the people in Gofa to whom she had been ministering that she was going to the conference, they said, "Oh, no, we won't let you go."

"I don't want to go and stay. I will be sure to come back."

"No, you are just trying to deceive us," they said. "You are not planning to come back."

Balotei tried her best to convince them that she was only going to the conference and that she would return again.

"You are going to leave us and you do not want to tell us that you are leaving," was the response.

"I'll come back," said Balotei, "I'll truly come back."

But however she tried, she could not convince the people that she really meant to return. They told her that others had come and had gone saying they would return, but they had never come back.

"We will not let you go," they insisted.

"What can I do to make you believe that I am telling you the truth, that I am really coming back to you?" cried Balotei.

"If you really mean that you are going to return to us following the Wallamo conference, then leave your little son Desita with us as a guarantee that you will come back."

Balotei paused thoughtfully. These with whom she was speaking were all unbelievers. She had lost Persis. She had lost Omochi. Only Desita was left, her baby, barely a year old. Not only that but Desita was her only blood relative — and the unbelievers in Gofa said, "Leave Desita with us as your guarantee that you will come back to us."

Balotei's answer came with a smile. "All right, if that is what it will take to prove to you that I intend to return, I will leave Desita with you because God knows I really plan to return."

So Balotei attended the conference. At the conclusion of one of the services she came and stood before Selma Bergsten, her hands clasped together. When others had finished speaking, Balotei stepped forward. Stretching out her hands she placed a sum of money in the missionary's hands — her husband's faith promise of the previous year which he had not lived to fulfill. Traveling alone on foot from place to place, teaching the Word of God, caring for their little son, Balotei had saved her pennies until she collected enough to pay it.

When the conference was over, Balotei returned to Gofa. Her heart had been refreshed, and her determination to share the love of her all-sufficient Saviour with her unbelieving Gofa neighbors was deepened. Mother love compelled her to return as quickly as possible. And the love of Christ constrained her to return, so that others would experience His love too. She found Desita quite well, and the unbelieving neighbors were overjoyed to see her. She had kept her promise and returned.

The Gospel has now become firmly established in Gofa, where Balotei and many others like her faithfully served God at great personal sacrifice and hardship.

The believers in Gofa were interested in knowing where the Gospel had come from. The Wallamo evangelists who brought it to Gofa told them that it was brought to Wallamo by the missionaries from the white man's country. In order to show their appreciation to the missionaries for bringing the Gospel into Gofa, they sent a letter which said,

We do want to thank you for coming to Wallamo with the Gospel message. We want to thank you for bringing the light into our darkness. We want to thank you for working in Wallamo, so that the Wallamos could know the Lord and so that the Wallamo people could come to Gofa and give the Gospel to us.

They signed the letter,

> The church of the people who wear no clothes, or we should say, from the church of the people who wore no clothes, because now that we have come to know the Lord, we are all happy in living differently than we did before.

22 — Amonei

*Except a corn of wheat fall into the ground and die,
it abideth alone; but if it die . . . .*

— John 12:24

"**I** DON'T WANT TO JUST LIVE. I want to live like
Amonei lived."

So read the letter from Adjo's mother to Amonei's mother,
quoting Adjo's testimony. And because of Amonei, Adjo with
her husband is an evangelist beyond Kwoiba mountain. It
all happened in the wonderful way in which God works.

The Gospel is preached by life as well as by lip, and
Amonei and Shanka were the kind of living epistles of which
the Word of God speaks. As a newly married and very happy
couple, they went as missionaries of the Gospel to live among
the Shankala people in Gofa.

Not often does one see in Africa, or in any land for that
matter, a young woman who has so quiet and kind a personality as had Amonei. She had given herself to the Lord for
His work wholeheartedly and unreservedly. Her whole thought
was that her life be lived for the Lord among the Shankala
people.

207

Although she was glad to be there for Christ's sake, she did not find the Shankala women at all friendly in the beginning. She could not understand why. Though she visited them, they did not seem to show any interest in her, nor did they invite her into their homes. They would stand and talk with her just outside the door. Only occasionally was she invited in, but never very warmly. However, her own home life with Shanka was such that she was not unhappy. And they prayed together that God would help her find a way to become friends with the Shankala women.

As he visited among the people Shanka tried to gain their confidence and invited them to come to his home. When the men responded, they noticed the great difference between this home and their own. As Amonei served coffee or food they observed how friendly she was, how she respected her husband, how she obviously loved him. They noticed how quick she was to get warm water to wash their hands before eating, as was their established custom. In the evening when they came to call, they would often see how kindly she washed Shanka's feet and how careful she was in caring for any needs around the home. It was truly a happy home and this was obvious to all who entered.

At last the Shankala men asked Shanka if he would allow their wives to come and visit Amonei. He replied that he would be delighted to have them come. Amonei, too, was happy at this new interest and eagerly awaited the women's visit. The Shankala men suggested to their wives, "Why don't you go and visit this new man's wife? She is all alone. She doesn't have any friends here, and she doesn't know anyone. She will be lonely unless you go and visit her."

So the women agreed to go and visit Amonei. But sometimes they would come and just watch her. They found it difficult to understand her, and Amonei found it difficult to understand them fully. She also sensed that the Shankala women were not too well pleased with her.

Finally one day she overheard a conversation between several of the women. "If we allow Amonei to stay in this area, she will influence our husbands, and it will then be that we will have to do all the work even as she does."

Up to this time Shanka and Amonei had not realized that in the culture of the Shankala people the woman was the head of the house. In the evening the women would sit and rest, while the husbands would get the tobacco, build the fire, light the pipe and bring it to their wives so that they could smoke while the husband was doing the work. On the path the Shankala women walked ahead, smoking a pipe, while the husband followed carrying the load. As they visited in Shankala homes in the evening, Amonei and Shanka discovered that it was Shankala custom for the men to wash the woman's feet — never did the wife wash her husband's feet.

No wonder the Shankala women had said, "We had better not allow her to stay here. Unthinkable! We cannot allow her to stay here."

It took a long while, but it finally happened — the women discovered the true loveliness of Amonei as they visited in her home. They noted the tranquility and peace that pervaded the home of Amonei and Shanka. More and more they invited her to come and visit them in their homes. As she began to gain their confidence and interest, she would tell them what the Word of God taught and read to them from the Bible. She told them what the Lord had done for her and what a happy change there was in her life when she came to know Him. The women would listen — but they were loath to give up their former ways and habits.

The young couple continued to minister to their neighbors for three years. From time to time the Shankalas would show an interest, but it seemed to come and go. While the ministry of this young couple had reached much farther than they realized, there was no outward sign of a change or a desire to follow the Lord until close to the end of three years, when at last a few were won to Christ.

Following the birth of her first child, a boy they named Caleb, Amonei became very ill. During her illness, the women came to her home and cared for her. "What can we do to help this one who has been such a help to us?" they asked.

For several days Amonei was seriously ill. Then she died and her death was a tremendous shock to all. The tiny group of believers was bewildered. One thing was clear, though: Shanka would not be able to care for his little son alone.

The Christians said to Shanka, "You cannot keep the little boy here. You cannot bring him up all alone. You must take him back to his grandmother." This was in accord with a decision Shanka had already made in his heart. "We will choose someone to carry the little boy back to his grandmother," they added.

There was no lack of eager volunteers. Many of the women said: "Let me carry him. Let me carry him. Amonei has done so much for us. She was our mother. She was the one who led us to Christ. She was the one who taught us to read. She was the one who has taught us the little things we can do to make our homes happy. We want to show our appreciation to Amonei and to the Lord by carrying her baby back to his grandmother to be brought up there in Wallamo."

Finally the church chose one of the older women, reasoning that the honor of carrying the baby to his grandmother — two weeks' journey on foot — should belong to an older woman. She was overjoyed at the honor, even though it meant a long hard journey. It was a privilege to carry Amonei's precious little boy on her back.

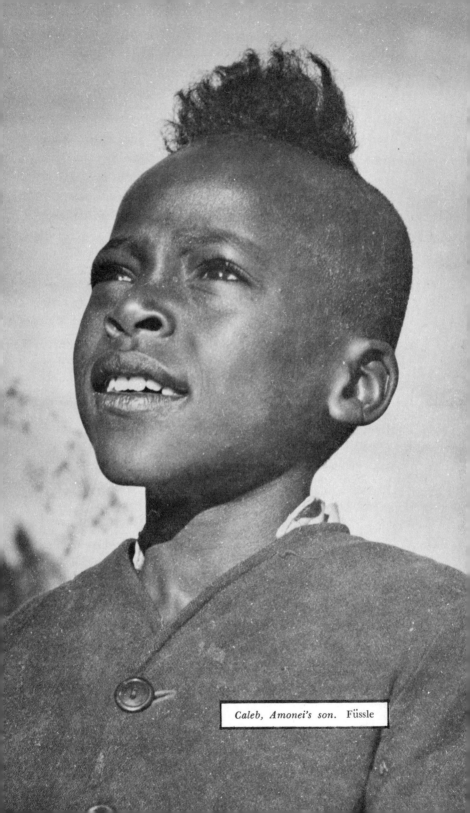

Caleb, Amonei's son. Füssle

When Caleb was at last delivered safely into his grand-mother's arms, he was nothing more than skin and bones, and his life hung by a thread. The long journey without proper food or water was almost too much for him. He did live how-ever, and is a fine young lad today.

Among the Shankala women whose lives Amonei had touched was a young woman named Adjo. Amonei died not knowing the impact her life and message had made. It is powerful proof of the miracle-working power of the Gospel of Christ that it was heard, it was understood, it was believed by these seemingly dull, unresponsive, unfriendly people. The Gospel was able to bring new life, new attitudes and above all the new graces of the life of Jesus Christ in them.

Eight years passed. The number of Christians increased. At the closing service of the Women's Conference in Gofa eight years after Amonei had died, Adjo's mother came asking if she might send a message to Amonei's mother. Her message was this:

> Will you tell Amonei's mother not to feel sorry because she allowed Amonei to go to Gofa with her evangelist husband? Tell her not to weep because her daughter died in Gofa. It is because of Amonei that I love Jesus today. It is because of Amonei that Adjo loves Jesus today. It is because of Amonei that Adjo's sister, Martha, loves Jesus today.
>
> Since Amonei died, Adjo has said, "I don't want to *just* live! I want to live like Amonei lived. I want to work like Amonei worked. I want to teach other women like Amonei taught us. I don't want to *just* live!"
>
> Do you see that far mountain? That is where Adjo lives today with her evangelist husband. She is teaching the women there just as Amonei taught us. Tell Amonei's mother not to sorrow because Amonei died here. The seed which Amonei sowed is now bearing fruit. It is now begin-ning to bear much fruit. Be glad you let Amonei come to Gofa.

23 ～ Gifatei

*He that goeth forth and weepeth, bearing precious
seed, shall doubtless come again with rejoicing,
bringing his sheaves with him.*

— Psalm 126:6

"No, I will not go. If you must go, you go
first. Then come back and get me," said Gifatei.

When Gifatei's husband told her of his desire to answer
God's call to preach the Gospel in Sidamo, she was rebellious
and refused to follow him. "You go out first, and then come
back and get me," she said. And so her husband went out alone.
He spent several months looking for a place to live and work,
before returning home to get his wife and children.

The day came when her husband returned to get her.
Gifatei said, "Well, I can't go with you. There are too many
relatives and friends whom I will miss if I go away for such a
long time. You go back alone. I'll stay home and take care
of the children."

The two spent considerable time talking over the matter in
a strained and unhappy way. She would not go at all and he
did not want to go alone — the early days of gospel work in any

213

field are difficult enough with testings and trials, without having to contend with loneliness.

Finally Gifatei's husband stopped arguing and went back to his field. He was away many months before returning. He hoped that this time his wife would be glad to go back with him, since she had had to take care of the home and the children alone for such a long time.

As he was preparing to go out for the third time he pleadingly said to his wife, "Now you must go with me. I cannot go and do this work alone. The Lord has given us this work to do together. You must come with me this time."

After some days of waiting and doing everything she possibly could to make him realize how great a sacrifice it was on her part to go, she said, "Yes, all right, I will go with you." But she did not really mean it. In her heart she said, "Yes, I will go, but I will do everything I can to make it difficult for you; I will do my best to make it so burdensome that you will be glad to come back home where we can enjoy life among our own people."

In the new work there were many days when food was short. There was no one near who understood their difficulties from whom Gifatei could expect sympathy. She found it easy to complain to her husband when he came home tired and weary from the villages where he had been preaching.

"When he was hungry and tired and asked for coffee and food," Gifatei told the Women's Bible class back in Soddo, "I would go behind the bamboo partition in the center of the hut and just sit there and not even look after the fire properly. I would mumble and grumble and take as long as possible to make the coffee to serve to him. I determined I was going to make it hard for him, and I did. I wanted to go back to Wallamo, to have it pleasant and easy, near to my relatives and friends. I wanted to have Wallamo butter. I wanted the grain that we could get at home. I thought, *Oh, it would be so nice to go back home. If I can only keep this up, he will soon tire of it all, and be glad to take me back home to stay.*

"Nearly every day I found some way of testing my husband. However, day after day he would go early in the morning and give the Word of God to many people who had never heard. He would spend the day witnessing to them in place after place and come home, weary and tired — oh so tired! When he asked, 'Is the coffee ready? Is the supper ready?' I would reply sharply, 'Ready? What do I have to work with?' Very often I would take out some dried corn and roast it. I would take quite a while to parch it for him, and then I would make the coffee. He would sit there so tired. Often he fell asleep waiting for the coffee. Then I, too, would just sit there and not rush the supper at all. When the corn was parched and the coffee ready, I would take it out to him, wake him up and say, 'Here's your supper.'

"Supper? That was not a supper, not even in Wallamo! That is what people usually eat at noon for a snack, but at supper time everyone likes a meal — perhaps a large plate full of sweet potatoes or corn, cooked on the cob. But he was never upset with me. He didn't seem to mind at all that he had to wait. He would tell me about the different ones he had found throughout the day, how he had witnessed to them. He was happy when they had really shown an interest.

" 'I told them,' he would say, 'how we had heard the Gospel, and that we had come to tell them about it, and they would listen very well.'

"He seemed so encouraged and so happy. I was so upset and angry. I wouldn't say anything kind to him at night when he could come home. He had left me alone all day and was out telling others about the Lord. I wanted to go back home to my relatives and my friends.

"One day, after many months, he brought a man home with him. He called out as he drew near and said, 'Oh, Gifatei, come meet the first one who has said he will receive the Lord Jesus Christ as his Saviour. Oh, come and rejoice with me. Just think! The Lord has given us the first one who has accepted Him as Saviour! Oh, rejoice with me; let us have some good coffee, let us drink coffee together — the first one in this difficult place!'

"I thought to myself, *Oh, my, now look at that. Here I have to cook coffee for somebody else besides you? Am I going to have to tire myself still more?* Within me I was just so upset — to think that I should have to make coffee for someone else too. *Was it not enough that I had to leave home? Was it not enough that I had to leave my relatives, my sister, my mother, my neighbors, the market where you can get anything you like? Well, if there will be many believers how can I cook for all of them?* And that is the way I felt all the time.

"So, I went behind the partition in the hut and started to make the coffee, but believe me, it took a long time, and I was grumbling about it. My husband was sitting out there beside the hut talking and rejoicing with this man whom he had found. Oh, he was so happy! They prayed together and they read the Bible together. They were very happy. And here I sat trying to blow up the smoky fire. I could not find joy in that.

"Finally, the coffee was ready. I took it out to serve this new convert and my husband, and that was when the Lord spoke to me. My husband was so happy, but not I. I did not have one bit of joy.

"The Lord said to me, 'Gifatei, don't you try to rejoice with them. You have no part in the joy that your husband has today. Don't you think you are going to find any joy in it at all. You have not sought for joy. You have not helped him.

When did you pray for him as he went out and came home
hungry and tired and footsore over those mountain paths, and
over those plains? You have no part in his joy. If you had
prayed for him, encouraged him, and given him food, which he
should have had when he came home — then you could rejoice.
You could say, "Oh, this is one that we have found because
I have helped in it." '

"But the Lord said, 'No! No, you have no part in this at
all. Your husband can rejoice and your husband's joy will be
all the more abundant for all his weariness, his hunger — but
you, what have you done for him? What have you done for Me?'

"By this time I felt so whipped. The Lord had dealt so hard
with me, I thought. I was just broken-hearted. I fell down and
cried before the Lord and before my husband. I said, 'Oh,
Lord, will You forgive me this one time for all of my sins in
not helping my husband as he was seeking to serve You? I
did all I could to hinder, and You wanted me to help. Will
You forgive me? Help me from this time on. I will give You
all my strength, all my love. Help me to show it in Your way
to these people here.'

"I confessed my sin to the Lord, and I confessed my sin to
my husband. Then we rejoiced together in the Lord that now
we were going to carry on the work together. Now the burdens
seemed to be light burdens, very light burdens compared with
what he had been carrying alone."

Gifatei was relating her experience to the women's Bible
class in Selma Bergsten's home. Every eye was on her, every
word was heard in searching silence. As she finished her story,
Gifatei said:

"Will you all pray for me? Pray that as we go again to
another new area I may go really carrying my share of the
burden, really helping my husband. Pray for us as we carry

on the work the Lord has given us to do together, the work the church here at home has assigned to us and for which they give their money to support us. Oh, pray for me, that I may be all that the Lord wants me to be, and that I may make up for those days — those years — when I was so mean and so unkind and did not realize the joy that could be mine in going out to serve the Lord."

24 — Oda's Wife

*Let us not be weary in well doing: for in due season
we shall reap, if we faint not.*

— Galatians 6:9

A GREAT BATTLE was raging in Oda's heart. He
would have to make his decision soon. What should he do?
How should he act at the funeral?

Oda and his wife were leaving their home to attend the
funeral of Oda's wife's brother. Although he was a Christian,
Oda decided that he would *not* identify himself with the other
believers who would attend the funeral. They would express
their sympathy in an acceptable manner, but he wanted to participate in this funeral of such a close relative in the regular
Wallamo way.

When they reached the brother's home, Oda turned aside
from his wife and joined the large and noisy group who were
giving uncontrolled expression to their feelings in weeping and
wailing. He helped in the butchering of the ox for the feast
and took his turn at the playing of the drums.

Oda's deliberate choice proved to be a great crisis in his
life. From that time forward he stopped following the Lord.

219

Oda's wife was broken-hearted, but she kept on praying faithfully for her husband. At the funeral, she sat alone. He was with those who were cavorting and carrying on, and apparently having a hilarious time. After a time, she arose and walked home alone to her children.

The time of death and the attendant ceremonies have always been a severe test for the Wallamo believers. The weeping and wailing ceremonies are so deeply imbedded in the Wallamo culture that it is difficult, if not impossible, for non-Wallamos to fully understand and appreciate them. Not only sorrow for the dead is involved, but courtesy, respect, social obligation, and identification with the clan. It is no wonder that funerals have sometimes proved stumbling blocks to those who are not strong or sufficiently taught, and to others whose hearts have grown cold. Such was the case with Oda.

From then on, Oda's wife had to carry the work of the home and garden alone. She provided the family with food and also helped a great deal with the clothing of the children because Oda now neglected these responsibilities. When Oda returned from the funeral several days later nothing was said. She did not complain or reprimand him because he had left the teaching of the Word of God and turned his back upon the Lord. She continued to pray for him. But as the days went by he showed no interest in the things of the Lord and went deeper and deeper into the old life. She stayed at home and prayed, caring for the home and the children.

Often Oda would turn to her and say, "You leave. You don't need to stay here any longer. I can get along."

She would reply, "No, I am going to stay here. I would like to stay right here and I will continue to pray for you until you come back to the Lord, until you get back into a life that you will enjoy with your family and with the Christians in the church. I will pray for you."

Oda was upset. To think that he had ordered his wife to leave and she would not go! Over and over again he told her to leave. Occasionally he beat her with his walking stick, but nothing seemed to trouble her too greatly.

"I will see what I can do in praying for you and helping you" she would say. "I am your wife. Why should I leave?"

"All right, stay then!"

It was not because Oda wanted to be alone that he had asked his wife to leave. He really wanted her to turn her back upon the believing way with him. But that she would not do.

Then one day Oda took his wife's best cloth. A cloth to a woman in Wallamo is her dress in the daytime, her blanket at night. She spends weeks and weeks getting the cotton, combing it, spinning it, and then pays a considerable price to have it woven. Oda took his wife's cloth to the market, sold it and spent the money for his own pleasure. When he returned home penniless and without the cloth she was deeply hurt. However, she did not say to him, "Why did you take my cloth?" She continued faithfully to pray for him and looked forward in faith to see the day when he would return to the Lord.

Nothing was too mean or cruel for Oda to do to his wife trying to make her angry with him. When she wanted to attend the women's Bible classes he forbade her to go. When even this did not upset her he took her cow. It had been given to her personally by her parents as a wedding gift. He took the cow to market and sold it. When he came home he said nothing of what he had done.

But his wife made no mention of the cow, or asked what he had done with it. By this time Oda was almost beside himself. Try as he would he simply could not make her angry so that she would start fighting with him.

"I can't see why you go on loving me," he said. "I don't want it. I can't stand it. I will not tolerate you for another day with your patience and kindness!"

But the Lord whom Oda's wife loved gave her the grace and patience she needed. Oda tried many different ways to get rid of her — but without success.

Finally, Oda decided that he would try one more thing — he married another wife. When he brought her into the little compound, he said in a voice loud enough for all to hear, "Now this is your home."

Oda's first wife observed it all, but still she did not get angry with Oda. "I will continue to pray for you," she said, and stayed on working and caring for the children. As day after day passed Oda expectantly anticipated trouble between the two women. He thought, *She will surely get upset with that other woman living here in her home. No house is big enough for two women.*

Week after week passed but nothing happened. Every time he came home he would see the two women talking. He noted that his first wife was kind to the new wife, that she was witnessing to her.

Then one day Oda came home to find his second wife was ill. His first thought was, *Oh good, this will do it. My first wife will certainly not be willing to wait upon her without getting angry.* Night after night he returned home from the field and the markets, hoping. But to his consternation, he found his first wife was just as kind to his second wife as she could possibly be.

Finally, it happened! No, his first wife didn't leave. But his second wife began to believe just as his first wife did. That made Oda so angry that he sent the second wife away. How maddening that a first wife should have more influence upon a second wife than her husband did!

Somehow this proved to be too much for Oda. He came to his wife and said, "Because of your patience, your kindness, your long-suffering and your love, I am coming back to the Lord today." He asked his wife's forgiveness and then made all his action known to the elders of the church. In their presence he fell on his face before the Lord and poured out his heart for forgiveness for the way he had walked since he first turned aside, for the deep sin into which he had gone, and the way in which he had mistreated his family.

The following Sunday Oda and his wife came to church together with their family. By her steadfastness, her faithfulness to her husband and her earnest prayers, he was restored.

25 ~ Laffamey

He which soweth sparingly shall reap also sparingly; and he which soweth bountifully shall reap also bountifully.

— II Corinthians 9:6

"YES, LORD, I will give you my cow, but — !" Sitting on the grass with hundreds of others around her, Laffamey listened. Her heart responded to the challenge to give her cow to the Lord — but it was all she owned.

Laffamey and her husband had responded to God's call to go into the southwestern mountains of Gofa to work among its needy and neglected people. Her husband had already gone ahead to find a place where they might locate, to build a house and plant a garden. Meanwhile Laffamey stayed at home, caring for the children, and getting things ready for her husband's return.

During this period the time came for the Annual Bible Conference at Soddo, which was a long day's journey from her home. It was not easy for Laffamey to get away but the Lord helped her arrange for the care of the children and the home so that she could attend the conference. She was eager to hear the messages and to be strengthened and fortified for the more trying days ahead.

At one of the first services a plea for financial support for the evangelists was put before the people. Not many were able to give much at the moment — few of the Wallamo people ever possess any great amount of cash — but the faith promise plan enables any and all to give.

One after another they rose to their feet to make their promise: one promised a cow, another a calf, another a sheep. Many offered coffee trees in varying numbers. (The coffee trees given to the Lord would be looked after by the donor and the coffee when harvested brought to the church and sold.) Some gave half a cow because they did not own a cow entirely themselves. This means that they would sell their interest in the cow and give the proceeds to the Lord.

While others were making their promises, Laffamey sat thoughtfully, deeply touched and anxious to know just what the Lord would have her do. She did want to make a suitable offering to the Lord. As she prayerfully considered her own possessions, it seemed as though there was little or nothing of any value that she might, however sacrificially, give to God. Then suddenly the Holy Spirit spoke to her and said, "You may give Me your cow, Laffamey."

Among the Wallamo people there is a delightful custom. When a young bride is about to be married her parents give her a cow as their wedding gift. This cow then belongs to the wife as her own possession. The couple may eventually procure and own other cows but this one is her own. It is a most useful dowry since it is not too difficult for a busy wife and mother to look after the cow. The milk provides food for the family and when it is sold in the market place affords a few pennies for other needed things. Laffamey owned such a cow and had looked after it well. Now the Lord said to her,

Women and girls enjoy the conference fellowship. SIM

Cows share the protection of a Wallamo home. SIM

"You may give that cow to me, and see that it supports someone who has gone out to give the Word of God to a new people."

Laffamey thought about it for a few moments. Then she said, "Yes, Lord, I will give my cow to you. Surely Lord, I will give my cow." Others stood to their feet, giving their promises. As the hour went on, Laffamey spoke to the Lord again. "Lord, I will give my cow, but You know my husband is out looking for a place for us to go. When he comes back and takes me and the children and we go together, then I will give You my cow. Because Lord, we have to have food. We have to have clothes. Our children have to be cared for, too."

She arose from the meeting and went back to the place where she was staying during the conference.

The next day Laffamey was again in the meeting. Another call came for gifts to be made to the Lord. As Laffamey sat there on the grass she heard the presentation of the great need. She saw others rising to give their promises and she was deeply moved. Again, quietly, patiently, the Lord spoke to her and said, "Laffamey, give Me your cow." Promises kept coming in — cows, donkeys, sheep, coffee, eucalyptus trees, dollars. Laffamey thought, *Oh, they are giving well, Lord. I will give You my cow, but I will give it when we go. I won't do anything else with it. I will use it to get food, some clothes and the things that I and the children need.*

The third day came. Laffamey sat with the others and heard, "How many will give some cows? How many will give some horses? Donkeys? Money?"

Laffamey went outside and found some men from her area. She asked them to appraise her cow, so that she could knowingly say, "I will give a cow that is worth so many dollars." They said, "Your cow will bring twenty-seven dollars" (U.S. $10.80). She returned to the meeting and sat down. *Twenty-*

seven dollars — twenty-seven dollars! That would buy a dress for me. It would buy my husband a new coat. The children would have something too. There would be food. Oh, we could do a lot with that! Yes, Lord, I will give it to You. When we go, I will give it to You. But not now, because we need it so much.

At the conclusion of the meeting Laffamey left without having promised her cow publicly. She had debated and discussed with the Lord as to when to obey — and she had decided not to obey right then. She wondered, when should she really obey? When other promises were made at the next meeting, Laffamey sat still. It seemed as though she was rooted to the spot. She just could not rise to her feet.

Not many days later Laffamey's angry neighbor, not a Christian, stood before the door of her little house shouting angrily, "Your cow has eaten my grain. You must come with me to the judge. We will see how much you will have to pay in damage for this." It was true. Laffamey's cow had broken loose from where she had put it to pasture and had entered into the neighbor's field nearby.

There was nothing for Laffamey to do but to go with him to the judge. When the judge said, "Where is the cow?" Laffamey and the cow appeared before the judge.

"How much grain did the cow eat?" he asked.

The neighbor said, "It ate a great amount of my grain and she must repay me for it." The judge put off pronouncing judgment, as is usually the case, and said, "You both come back in fifteen days and we will hear your case again."

After fifteen days Laffamey and the cow returned to court. The judge questioned them again. The neighbor was still angry, perhaps a little more so after the long procedure in court. Then the judge said, "Well, this is too great a matter to be settled today. You will have to come back again in fifteen days. Perhaps then we will see what can be done with the cow."

So Laffamey and the cow returned home. Fifteen days later they appeared once more before the judge. But there was still no settlement, and the procedure was repeated over and over.

When the judge finally pronounced his verdict he said, "This cow is guilty. It has eaten so much grain that it must be paid for." But not only would Laffamey have to pay for the grain the cow had eaten, she would have to pay the cost of the court action as well. All told it would amount to — 27 dollars.

Laffamey's little world crashed down around her shoulders. "Just the exact amount that the elders of the village said my cow would bring when I give it to the Lord," cried Laffamey bitterly.

Laffamey went back home in a daze. *Where will I ever get 27 dollars to pay the judge and the farmer?* She certainly did not have 27 dollars of her own. She sold every piece of clothing she could do without. She went to her neighbors and borrowed the remainder of the money. When finally she had gathered the 27 dollars she had not only impoverished herself but was deeply in debt to her friends.

One morning, not long after, as Laffamey awakened, she looked in the dim early light to the place in their one room house where the cow was kept. But something was wrong. In the night her cow had died. There it lay, motionless, absolutely worthless.

Laffamey sank down upon the earthen floor of her humble home, her head in her hands, crying as though her heart would break. Over and over she repeated, "Would to God that I had given Him my cow when He asked me for it. Now no new dress, no new coat for my husband, no new clothes for the children, nothing with which to repay my debt to my neighbors. And worse than all — no cow to give to my Lord."

Later, Laffamey stood in the midst of the believers in the church and told what had happened. "I tell this story to you, my people, for just one reason. It is that when God asks you to do something for Him, you must do it immediately. You should not think that you can bargain with God. You can't choose for yourself something better than He has asked of you. When God asks you to give something, anything, to Him, do it. Do it right then and you will be glad you did. Don't make the mistake I made."

PART VIII
THE FIRE STILL BURNS

26 ~ The Wallamo Church Today

> . . . I will build my church; and the gates of hell
> shall not prevail against it.
>
> — Matthew 16:18

T HE CHURCH and its ministry is today the center
of Wallamo Christian consciousness and way of life. In the
thirty years since Christianity was introduced, there has been
a complete adaptation of the Wallamos' social and cultural
life to this new way.

The changes have been made in almost every area of life.
For instance, word expressions have changed among the Christians. The customary Wallamo greeting to a friend who has
experienced some misfortune is "May it eat me," expressing
sympathy and the desire that the trouble becomes one's own.
Asked why they no longer use this expression, the Christians
said, "We stopped saying it because it wasn't true, it was a
lie. We did not really want the trouble to become ours. Now
we say, 'May God help you.'"

For as long as their collective memory goes back, Wallamos
have had the custom of burning a small patch on each temple
of every baby. The burn leaves a scar about the size of a

233

thumb nail. If a baby did not have any scars beside his eyes, they believed he would never have good eyesight. The Christians no longer do this and anyone who might be tempted to knows that he will come under church discipline.

The churches do discipline members who are not living consistently. The pastor and elders of each church are responsible for this aspect of church life. Whenever they run into difficulties they cannot handle themselves, they take the problems to the elders' district meeting for advice and help.

The organization of the Wallamo church has evolved to meet the needs of the growing church. There are eleven districts today, and once a month two elders from each church in a district meet for prayer, Bible study and counseling with each other about church problems.

From these district councils, two elders are elected to represent the district in the monthly "table meeting" of elders for the entire province. The naming of the "table meeting" is an interesting example of how closely missionaries are watched. After the Italians had expelled all the missionaries, the Christians tried to pattern their lives after what they remembered of the way the missionaries lived. The last Friday in the month the missionaries always met together for a whole day of prayer. And especially when they met for a council, they sat around a table. The church leaders decided they couldn't do better than follow this pattern.

The Wallamo churches are part of the Ethiopia-wide Fellowship of Evangelical believers, composed of churches from numerous other tribes.

Although the Bible is, in one sense, the foundation of Wallamo church life, in another sense the greatest shortcoming of the Wallamo church is its lack of depth in Bible teaching. Several factors have made this a most baffling problem. The lack of Scriptures in the Wallamo language is one factor, the

present regulation against literature in any language but Amharic is still in effect, so that for the older Christians this
lack will always be a hindrance. Christians grow best when
they have God's Word in their own language.

The phenomenal and rapid increase of believers during the
absence of the missionaries (and in later years), without leaders trained in the Bible, has resulted in great numbers of
Christians who have only the meagerest knowledge of scriptural
truths. In the last twenty years, emphasis has been put on
Bible teaching, and a great deal has been accomplished. But
with no academic foundation on which Scripture teaching could
be based, progress has been slow.

The desire for education has been slow in coming. The
general attitude, however, has changed in recent years, and
there is now a great surge to put young children into school.
For thousands of Christian families in Wallamo, there was
never an opportunity for the parents to learn to read. But
they are anxious for the children to have a chance.

The great surge in potential students has concerned the
missionaries and the church leaders. They recognize that the
provision of educational opportunities for the children will be
a major factor in the development of the Wallamo church. One
problem has been the facilities. The central S.I.M. school in
Soddo, which at present packs in more than 600 children,
cannot be enlarged. Nor can it be duplicated in other places —
qualified missionary personnel is just not available, and the
money needed for this kind of expansion puts it completely
out of reach.

A partial solution to the educational problem has come in
a self-help school program. "Why not start schools of our own?"
the churches asked. "We do not need much in the way of
equipment. Mud walls and thatched roofs will do for us."
Boys who had finished the four grades at the Soddo School

Soddo elementary school children line up for drill. Füssle

Wallamo young people listen and learn. Füssle

Boys are boys everywhere. SIM

Students bring their own stools to the local alphabet schools. SIM

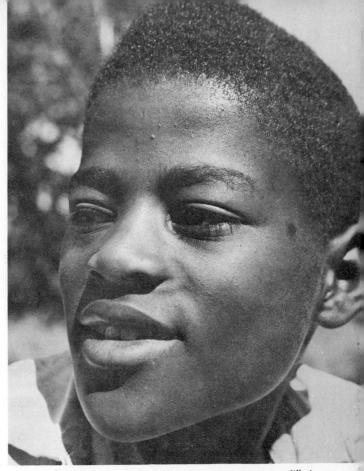

Füssle

Young people — the hope of tomorrow.

Füssle

Füssle

could teach literacy classes. Then, as they were able, the church schools would progress to teaching the regular government-approved curriculum. The churches with the missionaries agreed that when all the church schools were teaching grade one, the Soddo School would drop grade one and add grade five — and so on for grades two and six, three and seven, etc.

The idea took hold rather slowly at first. Then it suddenly began to gain momentum. Within three years the number of church schools jumped from none to 96. At the beginning of the 1965 session, more than 10,000 children were enrolled, with 115 teachers. Seventeen schools were teaching grade two as well as grade one, and five were also teaching grade three. Soddo School has added grade six and hopes to be able to add more in the future.

Now the idea has spread to Bible teaching. Twelve district Bible schools are in operation, taught by men who have been trained at the Soddo Bible School. As these church schools take over the lower levels of Bible study, the central school will be able to upgrade its courses.

So the battle against a lack of Bible teaching is being waged — and slowly won.

Wherever the Gospel goes, it creates a revolution. It did so in Paul's day — witness his experiences in Asia Minor and Greece. It has done so in Wallamo. In one sense, then, to bring the Gospel of Jesus Christ into people's lives, knowing its effects, is a kind of presumption. To bring bloodshed and suffering, pain and hunger and cold, even death — this is stern business. One must sit down and realistically assess what the cost will be to the people who will believe. Will it really be worth it to them?

The Wallamos say the Gospel is worth everything they have suffered. "We are so glad the Gospel came to us," they say.

"Persecution comes and passes, but God's Word and God's life do not change."

They would agree with Paul's assessment of the situation:

We are hedged in from every side, but we live no cramped lives; we suffer embarrassments but we do not despair; we are persecuted but not deserted; struck down but not destroyed; all the while bearing about in the body the death-marks of Jesus, so that by our bodies the life of Jesus may also be shown . . . .

For this reason we are not discouraged; but even though our outer nature suffers decay, our inner self is renewed day after day. For this slight, momentary trouble is producing for us an everlasting weight of glory that exceeds all calculations, granted we do not fasten our eyes on the visible but on the unseen; for the visible things are transitory, but the unseen things are everlasting.

— II Corinthians 4:8-10, 16-18 (Berkeley)

27 ∽ Why?

*The wind bloweth where it listeth, and thou hearest
the sound thereof, but canst not tell whence it
cometh, and whither it goeth.*

— John 3:8

*Not unto us, O Lord, not unto us, but unto thy
name give glory . . . .*

— Psalm 115:1

Around the turn of the century, Wallamo
province was filled with talk about a man named Asa. He was
originally from Gamo, but his fame and his teachings spread
throughout the whole area. He claimed to have a revelation
from God — the God who created the heavens and the earth.
Wallamo people should stop worshiping Satan, he said, and
should worship only one God, the Creator. Asa also taught
the people to pray, especially on one day of the week, Sunday.
In praying he would dip his fingers in honey and flick the
honey toward heaven, symbolizing that his prayers were directed
to God, not to Satan. The code of laws that Asa taught closely
resembled the Ten Commandments.

As his message spread, Asa's following increased, and the

240

practice of witchcraft was forcibly restrained. Many of the witch doctors, who were actually priests leading in the worship of Satan, were converted to Asa's teaching. Others who practiced witchcraft did it secretly.

Eventually the movement became absorbed in politics and Asa was imprisoned. He died just a few years before the missionaries came to Soddo, and though the movement died with him, there were still traces of this worship all over Wallamo. None of the first converts had been personally influenced by Asa's teaching, but there was a widespread spirit of expectancy for a fuller revelation from the One true God. Asa had prophesied that the foreigner would come with God's book. He urged the people to follow the teachings of this book because it would tell them more about God's will for them.

In a sense, one can never analyze the work of God. Jesus talked about the working of God's Spirit in terms of the wind — you do not know its origin or ultimate destination; it blows where it wills. You can, however, discover the wind's effects and you can hear its sound.

To the question, "Why did all this happen in Wallamo?" the ultimate answer is a mystery. The growth of the church and the effectiveness of the Gospel in Wallamo can only be attributed to the work of the Holy Spirit. The problems, difficulties, persecutions, short-comings — all these say that what has happened in Wallamo could never have been produced by mere human effort, however devoted and consecrated.

At the same time there are factors that one can discover, effects of the wind that can be observed. When we try to trace out the pattern of God's working, we do not minimize His sovereign grace — we magnify it. As those who are responsible, under God, for the development of a successful strategy of world evangelization, we owe it to God, to the church, to the world, to discover the means God used in Wallamo.

What we have seen in Wallamo (and are seeing today in many places in Ethiopia) must not necessarily be considered an extraordinary manifestation of God's power. It is a continuation of the story of Christ's Church, begun in the first century A.D., to be concluded when Jesus Christ returns to take His Church to Himself. What is unique about Christianity among the Wallamos is that in this place, at this time, God brought many factors together that would produce this kind of a movement. In southern Ethiopia God created a channel through which His power could be displayed in extra measure.

God uses everything for His purposes. Tribal and individual characteristics of personality, social structure, political organization, religious deterioration — all of these are discernible factors in the growth of the Wallamo church.

Basically the Wallamos are a simple, industrious and energetic people. Like all of the other Galla tribespeople of southern Ethiopia they were subjugated by the Amhara kings of the past several centuries, under whose rule the socio-economic system was a feudal serfdom. The Wallamo family of peoples tend to be submissive and were much sought as slaves. (Neighboring tribes, such as the Kambattas and Sidamos, were more individualistic and independent and did not make good slaves.) This is not meant to be a derogatory statement. Submission is a commendable characteristic from the Christian standpoint.

The social, political and cultural subjugation of the Wallamos drove them to find release in the spiritual realm. For as long as they can remember, the Wallamos have had an elaborate and rigid system of ancestral and spirit worship culminating in actual worship of Satan. But at the beginning of this century, the system was greatly weakened by Asa's strong preaching. With the religious practices of the past interrupted and the ritualistic religion of the Orthodox Church unable to provide spiritual solace, an ideal atmosphere was created for the coming of the Gospel.

And so the missionaries came — but only for nine years. Yet those years were comparatively peaceful ones politically. Even though a good part of the time was spent in learning the language and the growth of the church was slow, there were signs of an imminent spiritual awakening when the missionaries had to leave. Looking back they could see them more clearly, though at the time they were not fully recognized.

One of the more important factors which contributed greatly to later success was the carefulness with which the first Christians were examined before baptism. Out of a possible twenty-three believers, sixteen presented themselves for examination and only ten were actually baptized.

Now, after more than thirty years, only one of the original ten has turned back. The value of a clear-cut break with the old life as a requirement for a valid testimony in baptism cannot be overestimated. Most of those who were deferred later followed through and were baptized.

In distinction from other similar widespread movements where the distinguishing feature was group conversion, this turning to Christ was and is an individual one, involving vital, personal commitment. There have been the inevitable problems. Families were divided, husbands from wives, children from parents. Participation in the movement required the costly step of coming out of the old life into the new.

Although this perhaps slowed the early stages of the movement, it actually strengthened the foundation on which the Wallamo church was built. By coming into believing faith as individuals, not as a group, the spiritual transaction with God was more real, and proved a great advantage for stability in times of persecution.

A significant factor was the ability of the early missionaries to identify themselves with the people without Westernizing them. The Wallamos were almost completely untouched and unspoiled by outside influence. The missionaries always emphasized that they were bringing "God's matter" to them. "God's matter" was the principle area of common ground; it did not need to compete with other (Western) things for their attention.

From the very beginning stress was laid on Bible teaching, even though it was always a difficult task because of the language problem. The Scriptures were given their rightful place at the center of all life and work. The Wallamos displayed a great capacity for simple, childlike faith, and they have continuously showed an unusual readiness to obey whatever they found in the Word of God. Strict and persistent discipline, with and without the missionary, has maintained the purity of the church.

The Christians' zeal and energy for witnessing is part of the Gospel's success in Wallamo. They have not been afraid to speak openly of their faith in Christ. In fact their standard greeting now, after the usual "Saro, saro" — peace, peace — is, "I am a believing person."

Persecution has always characterized the Wallamo church. But they have proved, along with many others, that the more intense the persecution, the more their love for Jesus Christ increased. Even today it is not uncommon to hear a Wallamo Christian pray that persecution may return if this is the only way that their love for Christ may be kept warm and intense.

Even in the early days there was persecution when the believers broke with the worship of Satan, incurring the wrath of the witch doctors. The penetration of pagan rites and worship into every area of Wallamo life worked great hardship on believers who broke from the old way.

The Italian military and political authorities bitterly fought to suppress the church which they looked upon as a potential threat because of its size and external allegiance. The Roman Catholic Church, backed by the Italian occupational government, tried hard to draw the church into the orbit of its influence. When this failed persecution increased. The Orthodox Church has been jealous of the virility, enthusiasm and extent of the Wallamo evangelical constituency.

The church has always had strong national leadership — though none of them were physical, mental or even social giants. The leaders were and are common, ordinary men with an uncommon, extraordinary faith in Christ. This is what Jesus Christ envisioned when He "rejoiced in spirit, and said, I thank thee, O Father, Lord of heaven and earth, that thou hast hid these things from the wise and prudent, and hast revealed them unto babes" (Luke 10:21).

The willingness of the leaders and to a great extent the main body of the believers to suffer privation has also helped the church to grow. Repeated imprisonments, floggings, personal indignities and cruelties were borne courageously and joyfully. Scores of families have moved out of the familiar environment of home, relatives and friends to far distant areas to pass on the good news of Jesus Christ. In the beginning the evangelists were promised very meager assistance by the local church, but more often than not there was no help whatever, except as it came directly from God.

The warm love displayed by the Christians toward one another in the times of severest persecution made a great impression on the unbelievers. Since no provision was made by the prisons for feeding prisoners, it was the responsibility of relatives and friends to bring food. Believers in prison were so well cared for by the church groups — much more food was brought to the prison than they required — that unbelieving prisoners received the extra food. This kind of natural, living, unspoken witness brought many to know the Lord. Word of

The Strength of the Church

The church's strength is in age as well as youth, as symbolized by this old woman, Gutana Iya. SIM

Three brothers who suffered for Christ, Galazo, Garmana, Ganabo Godo. SIM

Three generations of Christians in one family. SIM

The strength of the church today is indicated by this baptismal service held in 1964, when 830 were baptized in one afternoon by 12 teams of 2 pastors. Füssle

such love, hitherto unknown and unheard of, spread far and wide. Others sought out the Christians to learn more of this new Way. When those who had believed in prison were released, they went back home and attended the nearest church.

These believers were an entirely new and different kind of person than most Wallamos had known. On one occasion the believers were not permitted to reach the prisoners in a certain jail with the food they had prepared, no matter how hard they tried. Finally one of the older women took over. She went to the prison authorities, saying that she had come to bring food for her brothers. Believing the prisoners were her actual blood brothers, they permitted her to give the food to the prisoners. When questioned about it later, she insisted there was certainly no doubt about the truth of her statement. "We may have had different mothers," she explained, "but we all have the same Heavenly Father, and there is no closer relationship on earth or in heaven than this."

The women played a great part in the spread of the Gospel through Wallamo. The strength of the church's witness was often due to the character of the women. They took the initiative in breaking down many of the old pagan and spirit-worship customs, instilling in their children the importance of the Gospel and the absolute necessity of standing true to Christ no matter what the cost. These simple unlettered women (few could read) stood faithfully with the men through severe persecution, comforting and encouraging them. Like the men, they did everything wholeheartedly. Just as they had followed the old ways completely, so now they were as firm in following Christ.

From the beginning of the work, the Wallamos were taught that the church, under the direction of the Holy Spirit, was a Wallamo enterprise. Of course, the first teaching of the Gospel came through the missionary. But as soon as there were

believers, they were challenged to be responsible for sharing
the good news of salvation with their own people. The process
of evangelism became the missionary teaching the Scriptures to
the believers, the believers passing on immediately and repeatedly what they had learned, forming in the Wallamo church
the unquestioned responsibility of "every-believer evangelism."

An important factor in the consistent testimony and constant
growth of the church has been the character of the leaders —
both men and women. Again it should be emphasized that
these were not outstanding people. As in the earthly experience of our Lord, the men and women whom He called and
who readily followed Him were simple, ordinary people. They
were, however, men and women of great spiritual perception
and whole-souled commitment.

Today the church is well organized and guided by strong,
spiritual men who acknowledge the Lordship of Christ. The
chief elders, appointed from all districts, meet regularly and
have their own headquarters. For many years Dana Maja,
who was once the slave-owning chief, has been their elected
head. His eldest son, Ato Markina, well-trained and educated,
is the secretary of the tribal church among the Wallamos and
has served on the executive committee of the Ethiopia-wide
Fellowship of Believers.

In these leaders is the evidence of the truth of the Scriptures:
"But God hath chosen the foolish things of the world to confound the wise; and God hath chosen the weak things of the
world to confound the things which are mighty" (I Corinthians 1:27).

Seldom does one get to see at close range and so vividly
the powerful working of the Gospel. Nor is one often privileged
to observe how God brings to focus so many factors — social,

economic, political, religious — into the "fulness of time" for the coming of the Gospel. The Wallamo church is a monument to the sovereign grace of God who produces in man His desires through the Gospel.

Tigyne, former slave whose freedom was purchased by the missionaries. SIM

Old and new in Ethiopia today. United Nations

Modern transportation has its hazards. SIM

Epilogue

Blessed is that servant, whom his lord when he cometh shall find so doing.

— Luke 12:43

During the two and a half years that I was in Wallamo, one of the young men working on the hospital building with me was Tigyne. Every morning before the work began, he heard the Gospel preached, and eventually he believed and received Jesus Christ as his Saviour.

But he was a slave. His master was very displeased with the step he had taken and would not permit Tigyne to attend classes for Bible study or reading. He also began to abuse him physically.

Frequent beatings and enforced absence from fellowship with other believers proved a real trial of Tigyne's faith. When we learned that for a price his freedom might be obtained, we talked the idea over with the elders of the church and decided that this would be a wise step. So several of us missionaries put together the equivalent of $12 (U.S.) and redeemed him.

Tigyne was deeply grateful for his liberty. Nothing was too great or too much to do for us to show his gratitude.

Then the missionaries were expelled. After World War II, some returned to Wallamo, others did not. Being deeply involved by then in the work in Nigeria, I chose not to go back to Ethiopia.

So it was after an absence of twenty-four years that I found myself back in Wallamo. This time, instead of a two-week mule caravan journey from Addis Ababa, we flew in, landing on the plain at the foot of Mount Damota. Waiting at the airport to welcome us were some of the first Christians, whom I had known. What a reunion, after nearly a quarter of a century! When I remembered the sufferings and hardship they had endured, I could find no words to express my joy at seeing them again.

Then we started the six-mile journey up the side of the mountain to the mission station. All along the road more Christians whom I had known were standing to give their joyful welcome.

As we reached the mission station and turned the last corner, I saw Tigyne standing beside the road. The missionary driving the car knew nothing of the relationship between Tigyne and me, and he kept the car moving slowly along the road to the mission house. I stretched my hand out of the window and Tigyne rushed over to take it in both of his and to kiss it again and again. All the while he shouted to his friends, "Behold! Behold! One of those who redeemed me has returned!" I saw that my hand was wet.

Finally the car stopped. I got out and Tigyne dropped to his knees, put his arms around my legs and began to kiss my dusty shoes. I reached down to bring him to full height and we stood with our arms around each other, while the tears streaked down our cheeks.

Later I was told that Tigyne, who has no calendar and

could not keep accurate count of the days, had come to the station for the past several days to be sure he would be there on the day I came. Since he had no watch, he had come to the station early that morning so he would not be a moment late.

This moving act of devotion expressed to me, who am only a man, seems to symbolize for me the love of the Wallamo Christians for Jesus Christ who redeemed them. They are willing to make any sacrifice for Him. And they are eagerly looking for His return, expecting Him to come at any moment. It is perhaps this quality of eager love for their Saviour that has made the Wallamo church what it is.

U.A.R. (EGYPT)

Nile River

SUDAN

Blue Nile

White Nile

UGANDA

KENYA

Red Sea

SAUDI ARABIA

FRENCH SOMALILAND

ETHIOPIA

See detail map

SOMALIA

JIM

GOFA